The Odd Duck Almanac

SPRING

SUMMER

WINTER

AUTUMN

The Mother Issue

The ODD DUCK ALMANAC 2020

BROUGHT TO YOU BY

odd duck

barley SWINE   *sour duck*

EDITED BY VERONICA MEEWES

ILLUSTRATIONS BY BROCK CARON   PHOTOGRAPHS BY RICHARD CASTEEL

Cattywampus Press

CONTENTS

LETTER FROM THE EDITOR................................ 12

CENTRAL TEXAS WEATHER PIE CHART 14

SAUCY ZODIAC PAIRINGS 16

PREFACE: Odd Duck Mother Sauces 21
BRYCE GILMORE & VERONICA MEEWES

Winter

Recipes for Winter...................................... 31

For the Love of Bread: A Manifesdough 54
MARK DAVID BULEY

Spring

Recipes for Spring...................................... 59

Mother's Little Helpers 81

Summer

Recipes for Summer 85

Farm-to-Table Partner: Richardson Farms 106

Autumn

Recipes for Autumn.. 113

The Origin Story . . . Or How It All Began.................. 134
BRYCE GILMORE

Drinks

Recipes from the Bar...................................... 143

Direct From the Mother Ship 151

Sour Duck Farmer's Market................................ 159

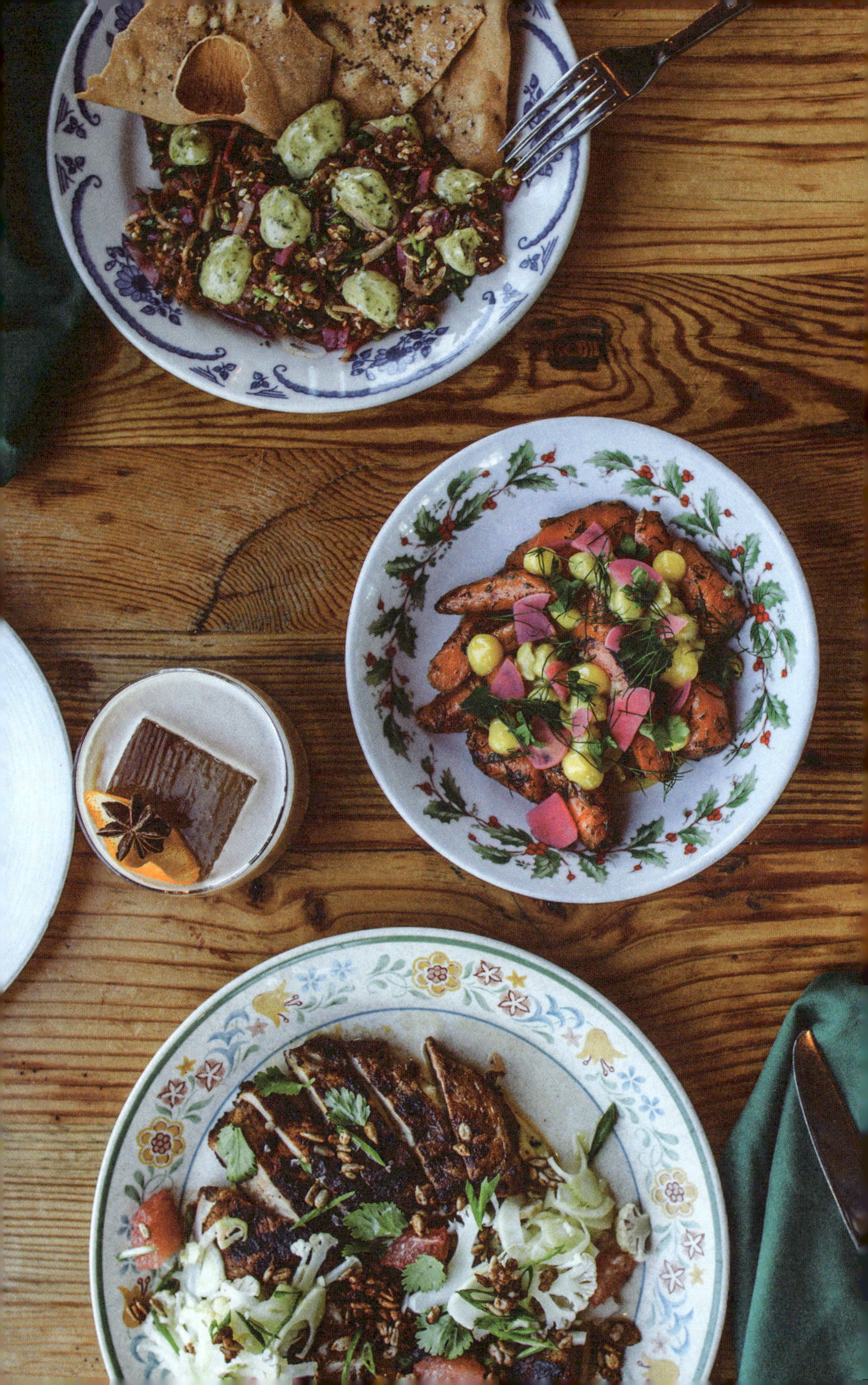

RECIPES

Winter

Fried Broccoli 33
    RÉMOULADE

Broccoli Quesadilla 35
    TORTILLA DOUGH
    BEER CHEESE
    BASIL MAYO

Cauliflower Fritters 37
    CAULIFLOWER HUSH PUPPY
    HERB YOGURT

Fried Fish Head with Beet BBQ & Citrus 39
    BEET BBQ
    SEEDED DREDGE

Squid & Turnip Slaw 42
    TOASTED GARLIC OIL
    LIME GARLIC DRESSING
    AVOCADO MAYO

Fish Tacos 44
    GREEN CHILE MAYO

TOP TO BOTTOM
Antelope Tataki
Grilled Carrots
Grilled Pork Chop

Grilled Pork Chop with Cauliflower & Grapefruit 46
    SUNFLOWER CRUMBLE
    BAHARAT SPICE

Goat Chili, Egg Noodles, Radish & Tortilla Chip Crumble 48
    CHILI POWDER

Carrot Cake Donut with Mesquite, Buttered
Pecan Ice Cream 51

Spring

Grilled Carrots, Lemon Curd, Curried Peanuts & Dill 61
    DILL GREMOLATA

Chopped Salad with Strawberries & Peas 63
    FRIED WHEAT BERRIES
    CHARRED LEEK VINAIGRETTE

Marinated Beets, Masa Cheese Curds & Black Bean Mole 65
    CUMIN VINAIGRETTE

Shrimp Radish Cocktail 68
    BOIL SPICE
    PICKLED DAIKON
    BEER BATTERED SESAME
    COCKTAIL SAUCE

Redfish Ceviche 69
    CILANTRO-LIME DRESSING
    SWEET POTATO CURRY

Antelope Tataki, Green Garlic Mayo & Rosemary Crackers 72
    GREEN GARLIC MAYO
    ROSEMARY CRACKERS

Roast Beef Sandwich, Pickled Carrot & Kimchi 74
    DANNY'S KIMCHI PASTE
    CIABATTA PULLMAN LOAF

Grilled Quail, Green Garlic Bisque & Snap Peas 77
  RAS EL HANOUT

Strawberry Baked Goods. 78
  BROWN BUTTER CAKE
  LEMON CURD
  WHITE CHOCOLATE GANACHE

Summer

Crab Pimento, Shishito Onion Dip & Grilled Potatoes. 87

Charred Green Beans Marinated with Tare & Togarashi 89

Pig Head Terrine, Hot Sauce, Fig, Pears & Crackers 91
  FRESNO HOT SAUCE

Shiitake Dumplings with Scrambled Egg &
Grilled Zucchini 92
  SHIITAKE CHIP
  SOFT SCRAMBLED EGG

Marinated Melons. 95
  CHILE OIL

Fried Quail, Creamed Corn & Peach Hot Sauce. 96

Summer Burger with Fried Okra. 98
  BURGER BUNS

Heirloom Tomato & Peach Salad with Chevre. 100
  SHISHITO PEPPER GOAT CHEESE

Sunny Duck Egg with Goat Sausage & Brown Rice. 101
  CHINESE GOAT SAUSAGE
  NUOC CHAM

Shishito Sorbet with Coconut Yogurt &
Mango Cake Crumble 103

Autumn

Smoked Fish Salad, Tostada, Apple & Fennel 115
    NIXTAMAL

Sweet Potato, Onion Caper Jam, Jalapeño Chevre &
Pecan Cookie. 116

Fried Shrimp with Tasso-Spiced Mayo & Apple Slaw 119

Grilled Zucchini Nachos 120
    CHORIZO SPICE

Veggie Chorizo Pretzel 121

Cold Turkey Quitter on Sourdough. 125
    HILL COUNTRY SOURDOUGH LOAF
    CHERRY BOMB DRESSING
    FRIED EGG PIMENTO CHEESE

Oven Roasted Quail with Oyster Stuffing, Grits,
Apple & Mustard Greens. 127
    CIDER GLAZE

Goat Stroganoff, Boiled Peanut, Sweet Potato &
Lemon Kale. 130
    ROSEMARY OIL
    PICKLE RELISH
    PEANUT BROTH

Rye Pecan Cake. 133

Drinks

No Brainer 145
    SPICY AGAVE SIMPLE SYRUP

Trinidad Jokes....................................... 146
    TRINIDAD HONEY

Paloma 147
    TARRAGON SIMPLE SYRUP

Salt of the Earth Cocktail 148
    BEET SHRUB
    TARRAGON & BLACK PEPPER OIL

Cory's Coffee.. 149

Whiskey 'n Cider..................................... 150
    CINNAMON & VANILLA SIMPLE SYRUP

LETTER FROM THE EDITOR

IT ALL BEGAN WITH MAYO, AS MANY GREAT STORIES DO.
When I first met with the Odd Duck team to discuss working together on a publication, they were set on creating a cookbook made up exclusively of mayo recipes. Anyone who regularly dines at Odd Duck knows they've made enough dishes starring various forms of mayo to make this a reality! We also entertained making a pop-up book with scratch-and-sniff capabilities but had to table those ideas while the team focused on opening Sour Duck Market.

When Cattywampus Press reached out about collaborating on a project, I had a feeling they were the type of publisher Bryce Gilmore could collaborate with. Homegrown, independent, and artist-run, Lindsay Starr and Daedelus Hoffman have worked on everything from artists books to cookbooks and zines, and always with a focus on the makers and shakers of the American South.

Guided by an experienced publisher, we put our efforts together, and you are holding the result of that teamwork. Part farmer's almanac, community zine, and cookbook, the Odd Duck Almanac is an annual publication that both documents and celebrates the culture and creativity of the immensely talented folks behind Odd Duck, Barley Swine, and Sour Duck Market.

When Bryce said mayo was one of Odd Duck's mother sauces (pg. 21), we began toying with the idea of a "mother" theme for this inaugural issue. We expanded this idea by redefining the five essential French cuisine mother sauces to reflect the food, culture, and climate of Central Texas. In the kitchen, the term "mother" often means origin. Bacteria and yeast play a significant role in the menus at Odd Duck, Barley Swine, and Sour Duck Market, where they are continuously spawning new batches of hot sauce, kimchi, and pickles. In the following pages, you will find many tips and tricks developed within the walls of these esteemed establishments.

Partner, Mark David Buley's "Manifestdough" (pg. 54) details how his entire bread program can be traced back to one mother— a starter he began cultivating years ago while in culinary school. In "Mother's Little Helpers," we visit Zilker Elementary's community garden program (pg. 81), partly sponsored by Odd Duck. "Direct From the Mother Ship" gives a glimpse into Odd Duck's vibrant employee culture. You may often hear restaurants referred to as families, but I've found that to be especially true behind the scenes of this particular restaurant group.

Farmer-partners are highlighted throughout this publication, including an interview with Jim Richardson (pg. 106), whose worked with Odd Duck since day one. Of course, this is but a few of the local farmers Bryce works with year-round, and all three restaurants showcase the fruits of their endless labor. They even started a farmer's market at Sour Duck Market (pg. 159) to help small-scale farms sell their goods with minimal risk.

I've been writing about Austin's food scene for nearly fifteen years, and seen plenty of restaurants come and go. I've also seen chefs talk big game without practicing what they preach; greenwashing is rampant right now in the restaurant industry. Bryce and Dylan Gilmore, Mark David Buley, and Jason James are, without a doubt, some of the most genuine folks working in Austin's vital restaurant scene. They're also passionate about cultivating our local food economy in the most delicious way, and it's been an honor to work with them on this publication.

VERONICA MEEWES

Central Texas WEATHER Pie Chart

WET

SPRING IS OH SO NICE! CAN WE GET A BIGGER SLICE?

WINTER CAN BE A BREEZE OR A TOTAL FREEZE

AUTUMN IS SOMEWHAT COOL BUT WE STILL GO TO THE POOL.

THE WET SEASON consists of Spring, Autumn, and Winter months. Things grow well during this season. 2019 saw almost no hard freezes in the Winter months, and given our current global conditions, we can most likely expect the same for 2020.

HERE IN CENTRAL TEXAS,

we have two weather seasons—wet and hot. This polarity significantly affects our local farmers and the varieties of vegetables they provide, which means we have to be flexible in the kitchen.

HOT

SUMMER IS HERE TO STAY IN A MAJORLY SWEATY WAY

FOLKS LOVE TO TALK ABOUT THE HEAT! Probably because Summer occupies half of the year, with many days registering over 100 degrees. The heat begins in late-March and begins to subside in mid-October. While patio dining and iced cocktails are lovely, a few more days of hot cocoa and the smell of slowly braised meat would be much appreciated in 2020.

SAUCY ZODIAC PAIRINGS

♈ ARIES
MARCH 21–APRIL 19

This confident fire sign, typically found tearing through life with guns blazing, needs a bold condiment to match. The initial intense burn of **HORSERADISH** matches the intensity of an impassioned Aries diatribe, adding plenty of spice to any conversation.

♉ TAURUS
APRIL 20–MAY 20

Though practical and reliable, Taurus also loves indulgence and decadence, making **AIOLI** (or mayo) their ideal spirit condiment. Both the spread—and this stubborn earth sign—can be polarizing, but keep in mind that Taurus, much like its creamy counterpart, only intends to make everything better.

♊ GEMINI
MAY 21–JUNE 20

RELISH comes in many forms, adding a sweet zing or a savory lift to whatever it's topping. An Air sign notoriously represented by twins, this astrological chameleon often presents a dual personality and is known to shift between the two. So while you may not know which side of Gemini you'll see when, you can be sure there will never be a dull moment.

♋ CANCER
JUNE 21–JULY 22

Nurturing and hospitable, Cancers love to welcome friends into their home and have a soft spot for animals of all kinds. However, this sensitive Water sign is ruled by the always-shifting moon, meaning their mood can change as quickly as the contrasting flavors of a punchy **SWEET & SOUR SAUCE**.

♌ LEO
JULY 23–AUGUST 22

Always the life of the party, proud Leos love to surround themselves with friends and admirers. This natural-born leader and entertainer is most content with a bottle of sweet and smoky **BARBECUE SAUCE** in hand. Ideally while operating a fired-up grill at a backyard party.

♍ VIRGO
AUGUST 23–SEPTEMBER 22

Virgos, known to be analytical perfectionists, may come off as stringent at first but are also some of the most reliable problem-solvers. Imagine fish and chips without a side of **MALT VINEGAR** for dipping. Exactly: you can't.

♎ LIBRA
SEPTEMBER 23–OCTOBER 22

This charming people-pleasing Air sign is all about balance and harmony—and what better way to bring people together than a ramekin of creamy **RANCH**? We all know that most things are better with a healthy dose of the stuff. Similarly, the world would be better off with more Libras.

♏ SCORPIO
OCTOBER 23–NOVEMBER 21

Scorpios are known to be one of the most passionate zodiac signs, but they can also be overly controlling and jealous. Much like **MUSTARD** (be it yellow, brown or whole grain), Scorpios might be too intense for some, but those who can handle this powerful water sign will surely be rewarded with a flavorful experience

♐ SAGITTARIUS
NOVEMBER 22–DECEMBER 21

This extroverted, open-minded Fire sign loves people, culture, adventure and change—a combination that often finds them traveling around the world in search of all these things. Sagittarius are undoubtedly the human embodiment of **HOT SAUCE**, spicing up the lives of everyone around them.

CAPRICORN
DECEMBER 22–JANUARY 19

Earth signs are the most grounded of the zodiac, but Capricorns in particular honor tradition and practicality. Therefore **KETCHUP** should, without a doubt, be Capricorn's condiment of choice. It might not be the most exciting sauce, but it is indispensable, depending on the dish.

AQUARIUS
JANUARY 20– FEBRUARY 18

Always one to stand apart from the crowd, Aquarians need a seasoning that matches their fearless and unique sense of innovation. **FISH SAUCE**, whether dashed over noodles or used unexpectedly in many amazing recipes, might be just the ticket.

PISCES
FEBRUARY 19–MARCH 20

The last astrological sign in the zodiac, dreamy and creative Pisces are said to be old souls. They are also one of the most sensitive signs, which means it isn't unusual for this Water sign to shed a tear or two. And they can break real ground when left to their own devices with a bottle of sea-salty **SOY SAUCE**.

PREFACE
ODD DUCK MOTHER SAUCES

BY BRYCE GILMORE AND VERONICA MEEWES

There's no denying sauce is the boss. When chefs Marie-Antoine Carême and Auguste Escoffier decided on the five French mother sauces—béchamel, velouté, espagnole, tomato, and hollandaise—they were instantly revered as the foundation of French cuisine and became required learning for culinary students around the World. At Odd Duck, we have developed our own "mother sauces," that appear in almost all the dishes we serve. They incorporate moisture, texture, flavor, acidity, and fat into each dish, but they also leave you wanting to lick the plate clean (no judgments here).

"WE'LL OFTEN MIX SWEET CHILES WITH SPICY CHILES TO CONTROL THE HEAT LEVEL OF A SAUCE."

HOT SAUCE

WE'RE VERY FORTUNATE in Texas to have a variety of chiles to work with in the Summer—from spicy varieties like jalapeño and serrano, to sweet Italian varieties. We love Trinidad and habanada peppers because they aren't spicy and have tremendous flavor, so you can eat a bunch without blowing out your palate. We'll often mix sweet chiles with spicy chiles to control the heat level of a sauce.

We make hot sauces a few different ways. Sometimes we leave the peppers whole, take the stem and seeds out, and submerge them in a saltwater brine of around 3% salt for a week or two at room temperature. Other times we'll do a mash, grinding the peppers and mixing them with 3% salt and then placing plastic wrap over the container and something set on top to keep the peppers submerged. This process gives the salt time to draw water out of the peppers.

For jalapeños, we might remove the stem, take out the seeds, and infuse with vinegar. Then we'll grind and ferment the rest of the peppers and mix both parts for a more acidic chile-flavored spicy sauce. After it cools down, we either put it in the walk-in and let it slowly ferment, or bring it to a boil to pasteurize it. Then we jar it up, but it needs to have a pH of 4.6 or less to make it nonperishable.

MOTHERS OF *INVENTION*

We try to save a little bit of unpasteurized ferment for the next batch of hot sauce (we add one cup to every five gallon batch). It kick-starts the ferment, because we're introducing ready-to-go colonies of the lactobacillus bacteria. When we use a previous ferment to get a new ferment going, it's a three to five day fermentation process instead of two weeks.

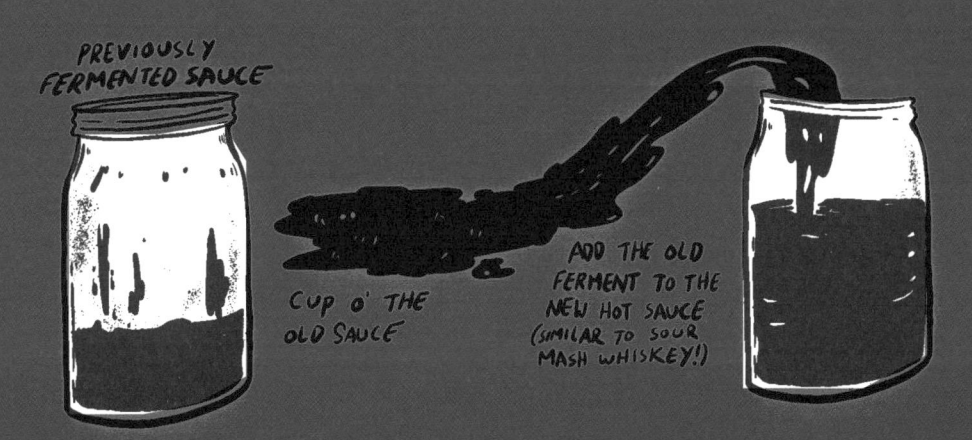

PREVIOUSLY FERMENTED SAUCE

CUP O' THE OLD SAUCE

ADD THE OLD FERMENT TO THE NEW HOT SAUCE (SIMILAR TO SOUR MASH WHISKEY!)

> "WE TOAST PEANUTS AND ADD THEM TO ONE OF OUR SALSAS TO CREATE MORE TEXTURE."

SALSA & RELISH

USING SALSA OR RELISH in a dish is a great way to add texture, acidity, moisture, complexity, and flavor. Whenever we make a chopped component like this, we want the flavors to blend so that even a small bite is distinct. Think of a pico de gallo, which is made of many distinct flavors—sweet diced tomato, savory onion, bright cilantro, spicy chiles, and acid, such as lime juice or vinegar, plus a little bit of oil. The oil helps all of these flavors come together and mellow out, transforming them into a salsa.

We usually start with a base of onions, herbs, acid, and oil. From there, we might add beets, carrots, peppers, or even corn. Mixing heavily charred vegetables with raw vegetables can also add complexity to a salsa. We even toast peanuts and add them to one of our salsas to create more texture.

For a commercial setting, a Robot Coupe food processor is most efficient, but even a nice mortar and pestle will work, plus it's fun to get physical. If I'm cooking at my dad's house, this is typically the tool and method for making salsa.

CHEESE SAUCE

IF YOU DON'T LIKE GOAT CHEESE, I feel sorry for you. It's something we're proud of in Texas. Goats thrive here, much better than dairy cows. While we have access to some excellent cow dairy cheese, the goat cheese we use could compete on a national level—especially the chevre being produced at Pure Luck Dairy in Dripping Springs. We use it whenever it's available, which is about 10 to 11 months out of the year. The other one or two months are in the late-Winter and early-Spring when they take a break from cheese making because all the milk goes toward feeding the babies.

We incorporate grilled green onions and garlic or fermented jalapeño mash, chopped and folded into the goat cheese. We then whip it in a stand mixer with flavored oil and maybe a little extra acidity if we want more than the natural acidity it already has. One thick swipe of this baby across the bottom of a plate is an easy way to elevate any vegetable dish.

Beer cheese is another sauce we've incorporated more and more throughout the years—as a bavette sauce at Barley Swine, smeared on a burger at Sour Duck Market, and in a kohlrabi beer cheese soup at Odd Duck. We start with a béchamel base, and then add a vegetable puree and use sodium citrate to help emulsify the cheese into the beer base, without a trace of grittiness. We use cheddar, Gouda, raclette, and goat cheese, and then we like to aerate to lighten it up and give it a different texture.

> *"ABOVE ALL, OUR MAYO IS A STURDY FOUNDATION FOR FLAVOR."*

MAYO

ONE DAY, Kevin (the Chef de Cuisine at Barley Swine), told a server not to worry about the difference between aioli and mayo because we only serve mayo. It's true, mayo is a religion at Odd Duck. Our mayo base consists of egg yolk, Dijon, lemon juice, sunflower oil, and a touch of olive oil. We also like to add about one clove of raw garlic, grated with a Microplane, per quart.

The oil we use is dependent on what flavor we're trying to achieve. We tried grapeseed oil but found that sunflower oil is more consistent. Olive oil gives the mayo a grassy, vegetal profile but most of our mayo variations are flavored using infused oils.

If we're preparing a couple of quarts of mayo, we'll do it in a Robot Coupe, starting with eggs. If it gets too thick while emulsifying the oil, we thin it down with a little water. From there, we've got an excellent creamy puree base to which all kinds of ingredients can be added—from salad dressings to pimento cheese spreads. This mayo sauce is also a way to incorporate fat and moisture into a dish, adding that creamy texture which helps balance the whole experience. Above all, our mayo is a sturdy foundation for flavor.

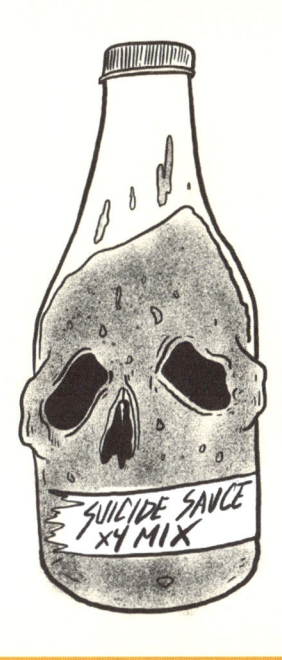

WHILE EACH AND EVERY one of these sauces is perfect on its own, don't discount the possibility of hybrids made from combinations like **MAYO** with **HOT SAUCE** or **SALSA** with **CHEESE SAUCE**. Or maybe even a suicide-style blend of all four? We're not knocking it until we try it.

MOTHERS OF INVENTION

Most of the flavored oils we use to make mayos consist of byproducts from the kitchen. For example, chile mayo calls for an oil infused with pepper scraps and stems, and tomato flavored oil can be made using tomato skins. We even make a "compost mayo" by using the items tossed into the compost bucket.

VEGETABLE COMPOST SCRAPS → OIL INFUSION → FILTER INFUSION → INFUSED OIL MAYO

ODD DUCK MOTHER SAUCES

> *"THE SWEET ELIXIR THAT SETTLES THE NERVES AND FOSTERS FELLOWSHIP AND RELAXATION AFTER A LONG DAY."*

WHISKEY

OUR FIFTH MOTHER SAUCE is *THE* Sauce. And the most superior kind, at that. Whiskey is the amber liquid that keeps the staff going. They especially appreciate guests who bring in a bottle for the kitchen to share later. They place it on the pass as a persistent reminder of the love we receive.

Working through the daily struggles of operating a from-scratch, farm-focused restaurant is tough. A myriad of issues can arise in a day, and this mother sauce is the sweet elixir that settles the nerves and fosters fellowship and relaxation after a long day. This crucial unwinding time is used to reflect on the day's triumphs and tragedies and to have camaraderie.

When Bryce was in New York for the James Beard awards a few years ago, Jason poured little shots for everyone to toast his win—but alas, he did not win. However, success is not measured by awards but by the smiling faces on both sides of the line every night. Jason called Bryce so he could hear the sound of the entire staff toasting him and the nomination with a shot of Balcones down the hatch.

HEAD'S UP!

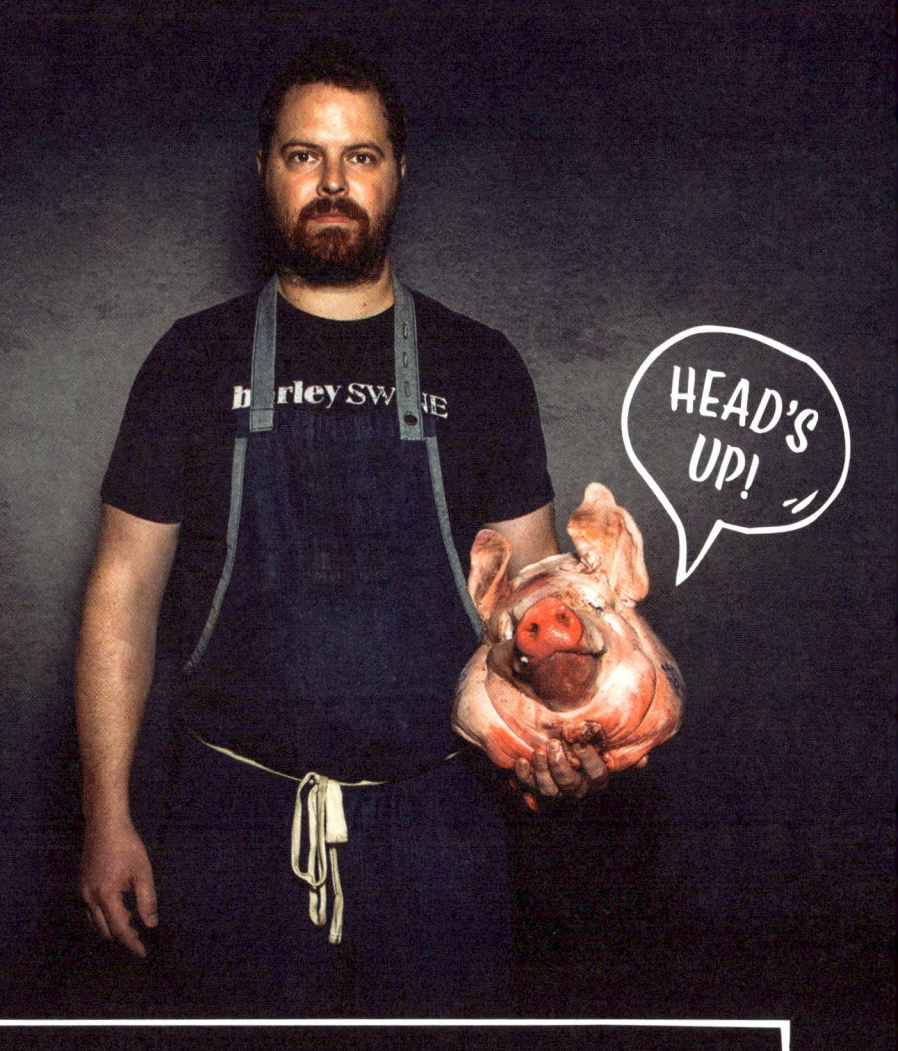

DISCLAIMER: These recipes are from our database and are inputted by various creators, whether me or a sous chef or even a line cook that had a good idea. You'll see different types of measurements throughout based on how we were feeling at the moment. You might even see something that doesn't make sense to you as a "civilian," and that's OK. Some of the dishes are more detailed than others, and some provide a concept that will inspire you to do your own thing. I hope this collection of recipes motivates you to check out your local farmer's market and get cooking! If you have questions about how we do things in more detail, you know where to find us.

FROM THE FARM

"BROCCOLI IS ONE OF THE MOST POPULAR WINTER VEGGIES AND IS LOADED WITH VITAMIN C, GIVING A BOOST TO YOUR IMMUNE SYSTEM IN THE MIDDLE OF WINTER."

CAS VAN WOERDEN,
ANIMAL FARM CENTER, CAT SPRING, TX

RECIPES FOR WINTER

JANUARY–FEBRUARY

WILD CARD WINTER

WILL THERE BE BLACK ICE . . .
OR ENOUGH SUN TO PLANT SEEDS?
TIME TO BUY NEW SOCKS.

WINTER IN TEXAS is more like Fall most everywhere else. For farmers, the stress of the past year fades away into a much-needed respite. As the leaves fall and the air chills to a crisp, they finally have a chance to fix equipment and start planning for the upcoming year. In these cooler months, we start using a lot of citruses, broccoli, and Brussels sprouts—all the things you associate with Wintertime. Brassicas (cabbage family) like turnips, kohlrabi, mustard greens, and cabbage also do best when it's cold at night, hitting their peak in January or February. We are lucky to have an incredibly fruitful Winter in central Texas, especially compared to other parts of the world.

FRIED BROCCOLI

SOUR DUCK MARKET

Remember when fried Brussels sprouts were all the rage? There was a time when I couldn't stand the smell of frying Brussels. The idea here is to fry the broccoli naked (just like you would for Brussels sprouts) to caramelize the florets and bring out the nutty, slightly bitter flavors. Plus, it's the easiest way to cook something. Throw it in a big vat of hot oil until it's crispy! We serve this dish with a heaping scoop of rémoulade.

RÉMOULADE

2 qt	mayo made with Worcestershire sauce
1 c	celery *fine dice*
.5 c	green onion or Spring onion
3 tbsp	tarragon
.5 c	parsley
3 tbsp	Dijon
1 ea.	garlic
2 tbsp	jalapeños and fermented habanero
3 tbsp	crawfish spice
TT	lemon

Make a basic mayo, using Worcestershire instead of water. Add a good amount of salt and lemon, then fine mince the vegetables and fold in along with the other ingredients. Taste and adjust with more spices, lemon, and Worcestershire, to taste. Mix equal parts picked smoked fish and rémoulade for the final product.

Scoop rémoulade into small "rice bowl." Fry broccoli until it has golden-brown edges (about 90 seconds). Drain from the fryer, season with lemon juice and salt. Place fried broccoli in the bowl on top of rémoulade. Garnish with broccoli stems and pepitas.

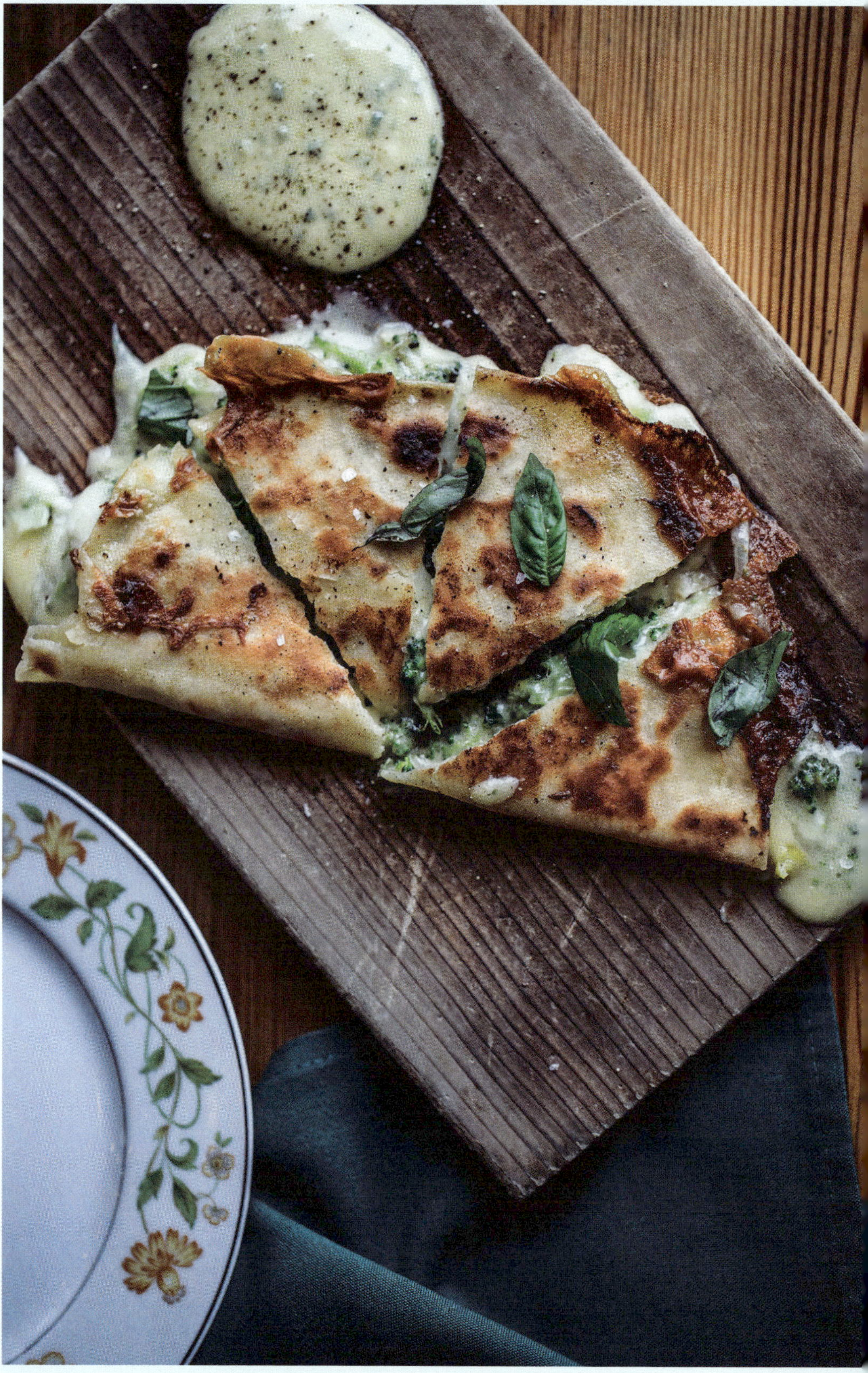

BROCCOLI QUESADILLA

ODD DUCK

I grew up eating quesadillas, Texas' version of a grilled cheese sandwich, at Tex-Mex restaurants and found them to be an easy snack to make at home. Instead of the typical chicken and cheese, we make this vegetarian version that will satisfy meat lovers as well. Make sure to butter each side of the quesadilla heavily to get a good crisp and golden-color on each side.

FILLING

1250 g	steamed broccoli
750 g	steamed and grilled broccoli stems
15 g	lime zest
75 g	white distilled vinegar
240 g	pickled onion
750 g	Oaxaca cheese
15 g	pickled jalapeño
25 g	mild fermented peppers
25 g	salt

BROCCOLI. Set up two steamers. Place a four inch perforated hotel pan inside a six inch hotel pan filled halfway with water. Top with a metal lid and place over high heat across two burners until boiling.

Once boiling, put the broccoli stems in one steamer and the florets in the other. The florets will take about six minutes. The stems will take about 15 minutes depending on the size. Once broccoli is steamed (a cake tester can pass through it with little resistance), cool broccoli on sheet trays lined with parchment.

While cooling, start rough chopping the pickled onions and mincing the pickled jalapeños. Remove the plastic from the Oaxaca cheese and tear into smaller pieces. Pulse Oaxaca in Robot Coupe until it's choppy and comparable in size to the pickled onions.

Once the broccoli is cool, Robot Coupe to the same size as the Oaxaca cheese, mix all remaining ingredients except for the ferment, and taste. Be sure to taste fermented peppers for spiciness before adding to mixture. Look for maximum chile flavor with mild heat.

TORTILLA DOUGH

1286.25 g	AP flour
428.75 g	Sonora wheat flour
358 g	butter
25 g	baking powder
19 g	salt
857 g	water

Weigh dry and fat ingredients in a mixing bowl. Reserve water separately. Using a paddle, start by mixing the dry ingredients on speed two for two minutes. Towards the end of mixing, stream water into the mixture. Switch to a dough hook and mix on speed one for five minutes. Wrap and chill. Portion to 50 grams. Boule. Spray, chill, and rest. Roll out as close to use as possible. Do not stack more than 12 tortillas and separate with parchment to prevent sticking.

BEER CHEESE

575 g	Zoe beer
70 g	sodium citrate
1250 g	cheddar cheese
750 g	Scamorza
60 g	salt

Grate cheeses. Bring beer and citrate to a boil in batches and whisk in the cheese, melting thoroughly. Stir in habanero mash. Season and pour into a Cambro.

BASIL MAYO

900 g	basil oil
55 g	Dijon
1 ea.	eggs whole
5 ea.	egg yolks
30 g	filtered water
23 g	salt
80 g	rice wine or cilantro vinegar
20 g	lime zest

Add yolks, whole egg, Dijon, salt, and vinegar to Robot Coupe. Blend until it becomes creamy and denatures the eggs. Add basil oil slowly. Adjust thickness with water as needed.

CAULIFLOWER FRITTERS

ODD DUCK

Most of the time, we'll have some sort of fritter on the menu. This recipe incorporates a hush puppy base to the batter along with cauliflower and curry spices. The yogurt sauce adds a refreshing brightness.

CAULIFLOWER HUSH PUPPY

4 c	cornmeal
2 c	AP flour
10 g	baking powder
10 g	baking soda
35 g	sea salt
150 g	onions *small dice*
300 g	cauliflower *small dice*
20 g	Vadouvan curry
4 ea.	eggs
3 c	buttermilk
2 tbsp	brown butter
4	lemons *zest*
.5 c	cilantro

Brown butter in a sauté pan, add onions and caramelize. Put onions aside to cool. Mix dry ingredients. Combine all wet ingredients separately. Combine zest, cilantro, and curry with wet. Sift dry into wet and mix to incorporate. Fry a tester and adjust seasoning. Store in quart containers with plastic pushed against the surface. Leave some space to allow for expansion.

HERB YOGURT

2 qt	yogurt
36 g	mint
45 g	dill
50 g	chive
130 g	olive oil
40 g	honey
10 g	red wine vinegar
20 g	sea salt
3 g	black pepper
3 cloves	garlic

Chop all herbs finely, Microplane the garlic, and mix together.

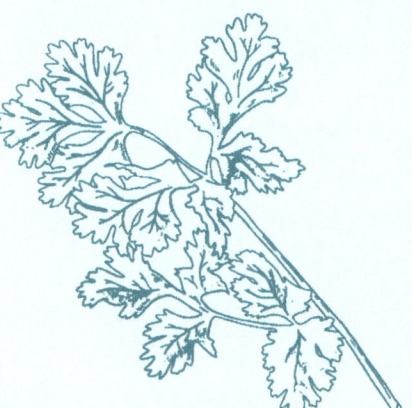

FRIED FISH HEAD WITH BEET BBQ & CITRUS

ODD DUCK

We buy a couple hundred pounds of redfish each week and accumulate a decent amount of heads depending on the size of the fish. A few years ago, we decided to sell the whole head as a dish and let people pick at the meat around all the bones and cartilage. Animal heads provide the best part of the animal. There's so much edible and moist meat that's full of flavor. Adding to the excitement, we dredge the head with spices and seeds to bring a crunchy, fried element to the unctuous meat.

BEET BBQ

75 g	garlic
775 g	green onion
1000 g	roasted red beets
200 g	brown sugar
400 g	red wine vinegar
705 g	tomato
120 g	mustard powder
30 g	black pepper
2 g	arbol chiles
5 g	cumin
4 g	coriander
1 g	celery seeds
3 g	cayenne
10 g	chipotle
400 g	pickled onion juice

Thinly slice the onions, garlic, and roasted beets. De-seed the arbols. Sweat onions and garlic until tender and add beets, spices, mustard, and vinegar. Cover and cook mixture for about 10 minutes or until everything is nice and tender. Blend and strain through a chinois. Season to taste with salt, honey, and vinegar.

PANTRY STAPLE

SEEDED DREDGE

2 qt	rice flour
2 qt	cornmeal
2 qt	white sesame seeds
4 qt	sunflower seeds
4 qt	pepitas
2 tbsp	kosher salt
2 c	sweet paprika
2 c	hot paprika

Sift together powdered ingredients into a bowl. Pulse seeds in Robot Coupe in batches until broken into pencil eraser sized pieces. Mix seeds with both paprika varieties, flours, cornmeal, and salt. Package, label, and pat yourself on the back.

FISH HEAD PICKUP. Setup a three stage dredging station—AP flour, egg wash, and seeded dredge. Roll fish head in flour, then egg wash, dredge—making sure to secure it to the head. Drop the head straight into a 350-degree fryer without the basket. Allow the head to fry for about 15 minutes depending on size. It should be warm in the middle, but does not have to be screaming hot or it will get hammered. We usually poach the heads ahead of time to ensure they are cooked nicely. That way, on the pickup, it's just warmed up. You could do this from raw and shoot for a 145-degree temperature. The fried head gets garnished with the warm beet BBQ sauce, salad of herbs, greens, citrus segments, pickled peppers, and onions.

"HEADS PROVIDE THE BEST PART OF THE ANIMAL. THERE'S SO MUCH EDIBLE AND MOIST MEAT THAT'S FULL OF FLAVOR."

RECIPES FOR WINTER

SQUID & TURNIP SLAW

BARLEY SWINE

This dish was created to be a light and fun start to our tasting menu. Squid bodies are cooked and sliced, the white turnips are spiralized, and the dish is topped with an avocado mayo, squid-sesame chips, toasted garlic-lime dressing, and cilantro. The idea is that the turnip mimics the texture and appearance of the curly squid, so you don't know if you've got a piece of turnip or squid on your fork. The chips resemble a squid tentacle and offer a light crunch and toasted flavor.

TOASTED GARLIC OIL

1 qt	grapeseed oil
1.5 c	garlic cloves
5 g	lime leaves

Blend three cups of oil with the garlic on low speed. Add to a pot and slowly bring up to toast the garlic. Once its light golden-brown, add the lime leaves and fry quickly. Add the rest of the oil to lower the heat. Cool down and remove lime leaves.

LIME GARLIC DRESSING

100 g	lime juice
40 g	Trinidad pepper brine
100 g	toasted garlic oil

Whisk together all ingredients. Put it in your ears and listen for the flavor train.

AVOCADO MAYO

300 g	avocado
70 g	mayo
50 g	chile vinegar
4 g	salt
1 g	ascorbic acid

Stick blend to incorporate. Rub on face before tasting.

SQUID CHIPS
- 720 g   clean squid
- 720 g   tapioca starch
- 150 g   water
- 28 g   salt

Robot Coupe until blended as much as possible. Run through a tamis for a smooth dough. Fold in half the volume in sesame seeds (very lightly toasted). Spread thinly in between two sheets of plastic wrap to fit on a half sheet tray. Steam for one hour and then cool down. Slice into thin ribbons and dry in a 130-degree dehydrator for about one hour. Fry at 400 degrees until puffed and crunchy.

SQUID NOODLES. Clean the squid and remove the purple skin with flaps. Lay flat on towels and lightly salt one side before cooking. In a hot pan with grapeseed oil and butter, sear the squid and flip after curling. Deglaze with water and pull out of the pan when cooked then cool. Slice noodles to mimic the turnip. Portion in cup containers, 22 grams for two orders. Finish with a pinch of cilantro stem and lime-garlic dressing.

FISH TACOS

ODD DUCK

We generally serve these throughout the year, changing up the garnishes with the season. My favorite way to top these is with a fresh cabbage slaw for texture. If we stay ahead on preserving chiles, we can usually spread some green chile mayo on the **TORTILLA** under the fish. We use redfish at Odd Duck for most of our fish preparations that are sustainably farmed in Palacios, Texas. I fell in love with redfish as a boy after visiting my grandma on the Port Aransas coastline during Summer vacation. It's a versatile fish, and the skin-on belly of the fish makes a great taco!

GREEN CHILE MAYO

6 ea.	egg yolks
2 tbsp	Dijon
1 qt	green chile oil
1 qt	grape seed oil
TT	chile vinegar
TT	salt

Green chile oil is made by steeping green chile scraps in grapeseed oil at 180 degrees, then blend and scrape through a chinois.

Chile vinegar is made by steeping dried chile scraps in hot white distilled vinegar. The final green chile mayo is made with a traditional mayo technique using the above ingredients.

> ## MAMA SAID
> Use the **TORTILLA DOUGH** recipe on page 36 to prepare a light and fluffy base for the redfish and slaw. The key to a good flour tortilla is to cook it right after rolling or pressing on a 450-degree flat top griddle

"WE USE REDFISH AT ODD DUCK FOR MOST OF OUR FISH PREPARATIONS THAT ARE SUSTAINABLY FARMED IN PALACIOS, TEXAS."

GRILLED PORK CHOP WITH CAULIFLOWER & GRAPEFRUIT

ODD DUCK

Most of our pork is sourced from Richardson Farms, although we also work with Peaceful Pork because this dish flies out of the kitchen! Pork loin stays on the menu most of the year, and we change the garnishes with the season. We buy whole bone-in loins that get brined for two days then held in the walk-in to age for up to two weeks in front of a fan. We then cut them off the bone and into 12-ounce portions. These get rubbed with a Middle Eastern-inspired spice mix before grilling. This particular recipe has a Baharat spice mix that we toast and grind in-house and keep as a pantry staple.

CAULIFLOWER PUREE

1800 g	cauliflower *thinly sliced*
160 g	onion *thinly sliced*
130 g	garlic *thinly sliced*
800 g	coconut milk
230 g	butter
10 g	Vadouvan spice mix
80 g	nutritional yeast
TT	salt
.5 c	sour cream

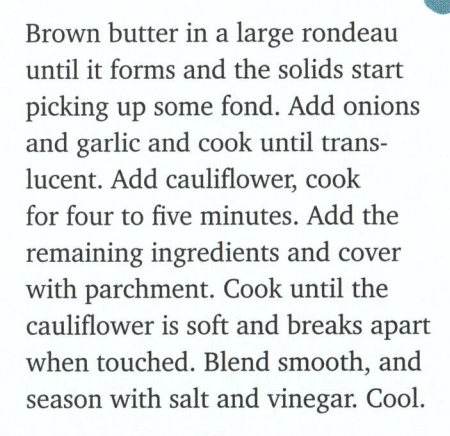

Brown butter in a large rondeau until it forms and the solids start picking up some fond. Add onions and garlic and cook until translucent. Add cauliflower, cook for four to five minutes. Add the remaining ingredients and cover with parchment. Cook until the cauliflower is soft and breaks apart when touched. Blend smooth, and season with salt and vinegar. Cool.

SUNFLOWER CRUMBLE

650 g	sunflower seeds
100 g	honey
25 g	nigella seeds
165 g	black olives *crumbled*
10 g	Baharat spice mix
1 g	vinegar powder
10 g	salt

Mix seeds and salt in a small bowl. Bring honey to a simmer and pour over sunflower seeds mix. Mix well and pour into a half sheet pan with a silk pad. Bake at 325 degrees, low fan for 15 to 20 minutes. Mix the nuts and flip the sheet pan around every five minutes to make sure you get an even toast. Be careful; the mixture will get super hot and sticky. Cool down, break up and mix in the rest of the ingredients.

PANTRY STAPLE

BAHARAT SPICE MIX

2 c	black pepper
1 c	coriander
1 c	cinnamon
1 c	cloves
1 c	cumin
.25 c	cardamom
1 c	fennel
2 ea.	nutmeg
2 c	hot smoked paprika

Lightly toast the spices except for the paprika. Toast until fragrant. Cool, blend, and pass through a china cap. Blend and pass a few times to get the best yield. Mix together with the smoked paprika. Bottle, label, and store.

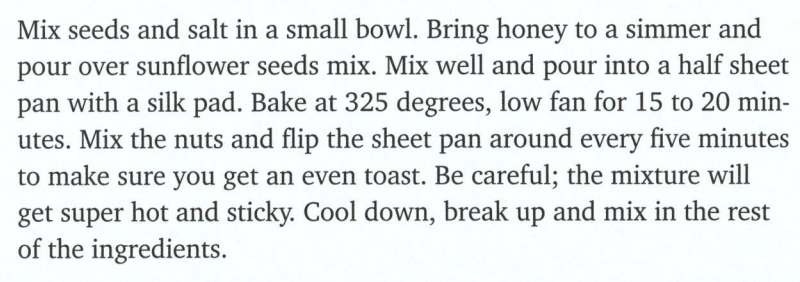

GOAT CHILI, EGG NOODLES, RADISH & TORTILLA CHIP CRUMBLE

ODD DUCK

We love goat at Odd Duck. It's flavorful and pairs well with other bold flavors. Plus, goats thrive in Central Texas landscapes and climate, loving the hot weather and rocky hill country. Windy Hill Farm in Comanche, Texas has provided us with goat since the beginning. More recently, we also started working with Hat and Heart Farm in Fredericksburg. The tomatoes in this recipe are sourced from B5 Farm in Lockhart, which grows them year-round. Jamey Gage does a great job with them, even when it's not Summer!

CHILI POWDER

2 parts	ancho powder
1 part	New Mexican chile powder
2 parts	chipotle powder
.5 part	hot smoked paprika

BEAN COOKERY

4 lb	pinto beans
1 tbsp	salt

Place beans in the pressure cooker and pour enough water to go one inch above beans. Stir in salt. Cook at high pressure for five minutes. Once timer is done cook for 10 more minutes. Drop the pressure, drain beans, discard water and cool beans in walk-in before adding to chili.

EGG NOODLE DOUGH

DRY MIX

4000 g	AP flour
2620 g	extra fancy durum
1430 g	Sonora wheat flour

EGGS
2620 g   whole eggs
900 g   yolks

ADD LAST
1000 g   water

Add eggs and yolks to the bottom of a 20-quart mixing bowl. Sift together flour and add to mixing bowl. Mix on speed one for two minutes the dough will be very stiff. Empty bowl into the tub and scale-out 5785 grams of the resulting dough add back to the mixer with the hook attachment. Mix on speed one for four minutes, stream in water (500 grams per batch) in the first minute of mixing, remove from bowl and hand-knead to uniform dough. Repeat process with the second half of the remaining dough. Sheet using directional dough sheeter to one millimeter, cut into 25 lengths, and store on a sheet tray with dusting flour between layers cut half inch noodles with wavy cutter and portion out into 70 grams each.

RECIPES FOR WINTER

GOAT CHILI

20 lb	ground goat
12 ea.	onions *medium dice*
15 ea.	garlic cloves *minced*
1 pt	pork fat
4 lb	pinto beans (sorry Texas)
1 pt	garlic-chile flavor bomb
5 lb	tomatoes
1 can	old chub
3 qt	goat stock
1 pt	chili powder
1.5 c	chile ferment
4 tbsp	cumin *ground*
.5 c	oregano *chopped*
3 tbsp	black pepper *ground*
5 ea.	arbol chiles
TT	salt

In a large stockpot, melt pork fat and bring to smoking point. Add onions and brown, add goat and brown. Add rest of ingredients except for the beans. Reduce for about 45 minutes to an hour, stirring frequently and tasting as you go. Add cooked beans right before finishing the chili.

TO FINISH

2 ea.	onion *small dice*
1 bunch	cilantro
1 bunch	parsley
TT	red wine vinegar
TT	salt

Dice onions, rough chop herbs and add to chili. Season with salt and red wine vinegar to taste.

CARROT CAKE DONUT WITH MESQUITE, BUTTERED PECAN ICE CREAM

ODD DUCK

This dish can be seen from Fall through Spring on our menu. Mesquite beans are harvested at the end of Summer and dried to be stored for the rest of the year. Its flavor is reminiscent of and complementary to baking spices so the carrot cake pairing makes sense. After mixing and resting, this cake batter can be scooped into balls and fried like a donut hole. We glaze it with maple syrup and serve it with mesquite buttered pecan ice cream.

CARROT CAKE

200 g	grapeseed oil
950 g	sugar
450 g	eggs
2700 g	AP flour
115 g	baking powder
15 g	cinnamon
35 g	baking soda
18 g	salt
10 g	clove
15 g	mesquite powder
5 g	nutmeg
400 g	carrot juice
600 g	carrot pulp *drain additional juice*

In the large mixing bowl, add grapeseed oil, sugar, carrot pulp, and eggs. Mix very well with your hand. Sift in all dry ingredients and fold together. Once well-incorporated, add bowl to mixer and attach the dough hook. Turn on speed two and slowly add the carrot juice. Do not over mix, for the donuts will become too dense. Package dough and let sit for an hour. Scoop into one ounce balls and fry.

MAPLE GLAZE

500 g	maple syrup
400 g	powdered sugar *sifted*
2 g	nutmeg
30 g	milk

In a metal bowl, combine milk, maple, and nutmeg, and whisk. Once base is made, slowly whisk in sifted powdered sugar. Taste, adjust, and package. Should be a smooth glaze that ribbons.

MESQUITE, BUTTERED PECAN ICE CREAM

1 g	milk
200 g	trimoline
200 g	glucose
1075 g	sugar
6 ea.	vanilla pods
60 g	mesquite powder
7 g	clove
115 g	apple brandy
3500 g	cream
500 g	non fat milk powder
40 g	salt
40 g	stabilizer

BUTTERED PECANS

125 g	butter
35 g	sugar
700 g	pecans
4 g	sea salt

Gather the pecans into a medium to large bowl. In a small pot, add everything else. Put pot onto heat and cook until the sugar has dissolved. Once all sugar has dissolved pour mixture over pecans and toss. Add pecans to a baking tray and bake at 325 degrees until perfectly toasted.

FOR THE LOVE OF BREAD

A MANIFESDOUGH

BY MARK DAVID BULEY

TEN YEARS AGO, I STARTED A RELATIONSHIP WITH MY STARTER. (SOURDOUGH, THAT IS.)

I started Carlita in 2008 while attending the Culinary Institute of America in Hyde Park, New York. Like most starters and levains, Carlita began her life as a simple mixture of flour and water. No more than a mason jar on the counter with equal parts King Arthur flour and filtered water stirred together with the handle of a wooden spoon and left on the counter for time to determine her fate.

    A breathable lid fashioned from a bit of paper towel and a rubber band kept out any unwanted visitors but allowed the air necessary for wild airborne yeast and bacteria to drift their way into the jar, bringing life to the mixture inside. Within a few days, the first bubbles began to appear and, with them, the promise of the possibility of sourdough. Within a week, Carlita was producing reliable fermentations with her daily feedings, and my first independent stabs at baking a real loaf of sourdough began to crystallize.

She has been a ride-along ever since, producing bread at every stage of the journey since leaving the CIA in 2008—at Depuy Canal House in New York, Patisserie 46 in Minneapolis, and BB's in Aspen. In Boulder, she is still alive at Oak, Acorn, and Brider restaurants, and in Austin, she's responsible for the bread at Barley Swine, Odd Duck and Sour Duck Market.

As chefs, we measure our influence by how dishes, techniques, and approaches spread through the places our journey takes us. Carlita allowed me to scatter Hansel and Gretel breadcrumbs that illuminate my path as a baker, sprouting new loaves along the way.

When a starter arrives in a new city, it needs to acclimate to both the dominant local wild yeast and variations in the locally available flour. Local whole grain flour contains all of the same micronutrients that local wild yeasts have evolved to live in harmony with. Whole grains containing both the bran and the germ of the wheat kernel assure that the local yeast has all the micronutrients necessary for vigorous fermentation.

But before producing these fermentations, the starter must pass the "float test," during which a spoonful of ripe starter is placed in a bowl of water to see if it floats. It is one of the simplest means of assuring that the starter in question is up to the task of pushing a loaf of bread to full volume.

Achieving this result in a new city or with new flour is almost always a game of simple reps and patience, allowing the starter to adjust to its new diet and new neighbors. In other words, location equals identity. Starters assimilate and adapt to their new locale via the microbes that inhabit them.

Shaping a proper loaf requires the baker to make an acknowledgment of life and understand the dough he manipulates is alive and will be in a constant state of change while he handles it. The baker must act with the knowledge that every detail of timing and touch will show in the final loaf.

Move with too much force and the resulting loaf will be tight and tough as if avenging the wrongs that shaped it. However, too little structure, or tension, and the resulting loaf will be slouching and spineless, spiting the shaping hands that were too soft to bring it the strength it needed. A proper loaf needs tension, but not so much that its structure tears and bubbles pop. A loaf's development requires a vision for its final form and deliberate intention to ensure it arrives snugly shaped and properly nurtured, ready to spring into its fully celebrated form.

A seemingly simple loaf of bread is a collaboration between the farmer, the miller, the baker, and the bakery it calls home. This delicious synthesis shows how local flora and flour form the authentic dialect of the loaves we bake: a manifestation of wildness.

> "A SEEMINGLY SIMPLE LOAF OF BREAD IS A COLLABORATION BETWEEN THE FARMER, THE MILLER, THE BAKER, AND THE BAKERY IT CALLS HOME."

Mark David Buley (L) talks with Blake Gardner (R) about important bread matters at Odd Duck.

A MANIFESDOUGH

FROM THE FARM

"WHEN WE FIRST STARTED FARMING, WE ATE NOTHING BUT BEANS AND RICE AND LONE STAR FOR SEVERAL YEARS. WE NEVER WENT OUT TO DINNER. WE DEFINITELY HAD TO SACRIFICE."

DAVE & KATIE PITRE,
TECOLOTE FARM, MANOR, TX

RECIPES FOR SPRING

MARCH–APRIL

SATURATED SPRING

CAN'T MOW FAST ENOUGH.
FEELS LIKE HOUSTON UP IN HERE.
TURN AROUND, DON'T DROWN.

THE START OF SPRING is filled with anticipation for the season ahead. The weather is goddamn idyllic. Wildflowers are popping up everywhere, if only for a few weeks. Strawberries are some of the first things to sprout, so they are usually a good sign of Spring. Root vegetables do really well this time of year before it gets too hot. Some farmers have beets and carrots leftover from Winter, or others plant them later so they grow all through the Spring. Alliums also start popping up—spring onions, sweet onions, leeks, and garlic. But Spring can also be a risky time for farmers because the weather is so unpredictable. If there's a late freeze in April when peaches have already started to bloom, it will deplete or even kill the entire harvest. A farmer can lose a whole crop if they're not set up to protect themselves from Springtime's extreme weather occurrences.

GRILLED CARROTS, LEMON CURD, CURRIED PEANUTS & DILL

ODD DUCK

A light and bright dish for the start of Spring, the carrots are steamed before they are finished on the grill and then tossed in a fresh dill gremolata. The curried nuts add a complementary flavor to the carrots and a texture contrast. I usually prefer my carrots al dente, but with the peanuts, the carrots cooked a little further work well for this dish.

LEMON CURD

4 ea.	egg yolk
12 ea.	whole eggs
600 g	lemon juice
400 g	sugar
150 g	unsalted butter
14 ea.	lemon zest
TT	salt

Combine lemon juice, sugar, and zest in a saucepot and warm until sugar dissolves. Whisk in butter until it's fully incorporated. Whisk whole eggs and egg yolks together, and while the lemon mixture is warm, slowly temper the juice into the eggs, being careful not to let the eggs scramble.

Once fully incorporated into the egg mixture, pour contents back into the saucepot and whisk on medium heat. Controlling the temperature is essential; if it gets too hot the mixture will scramble, so be mindful of your heat.

When you start to see the curd form, pull it off the heat and keep whisking. Whisk in butter until it's fully incorporated and then season to taste. Strain through a chinois to remove any scrambled egg, cover with plastic film.

CURRIED PEANUTS

2.5 qt	coconut milk
1 pt	water
60 g	ginger
30 g	lemongrass
2 qt	peanuts
.75 c	Vadouvan spice mix

Add all components to a large stock pot and simmer for an hour. Once peanuts are tender, take out the ginger and lemongrass and season to taste with salt. Ginger and lemongrass can be cut into large pieces so they're easy to pull out when the peanuts are finished.

DILL GREMOLATA

40 g	parsley *chopped*
620 g	evoo
6 g	salt
6 ea.	lemon zest
24 g	garlic
160 g	dill *chopped*

Add all components to a mixing bowl and fold together with a spatula until a paste forms.

CHOPPED SALAD WITH STRAWBERRIES & PEAS

ODD DUCK

We've always had a salad on the menu for lunch. This year we decided to make it a big ass salad that someone can fill up on— not usually our style. We use shredded smoked chicken from Sour Duck Market and warm it up on the flat top to order.

The salad is a mixture of chopped romaine, cabbage, radish and pickled onion. The garnishes can be whatever you want, but here is what we like to do in the Spring, strawberries, grilled snap peas, B5 Farms tomatoes, goat feta from Pure Luck, fried wheat berries, and a charred leek vinaigrette.

FRIED WHEAT BERRIES. We buy wheat berries from Richardson Farms and Barton Springs Mill. We start by rinsing the berries and then pressure cook with two parts water and one part berries for one hour. Strain and layout the wheat berries to cool down and dry. Fry at 400 degrees until they stop popping, and the bubbles start to dissipate. Make sure they are crunchy all the way and season with fine sea salt. At this point, you could also add spices if you want (I like smoked paprika). Make sure you don't fry too long because they burn easily.

CHARRED LEEK VINAIGRETTE

200 g	leeks
8 ea.	garlic cloves
75g	Dijon
5 ea.	lemon zest
150 g	lemon juice
100 g	red wine vinegar
700g	oil
1 g	xanthan gum
TT	salt

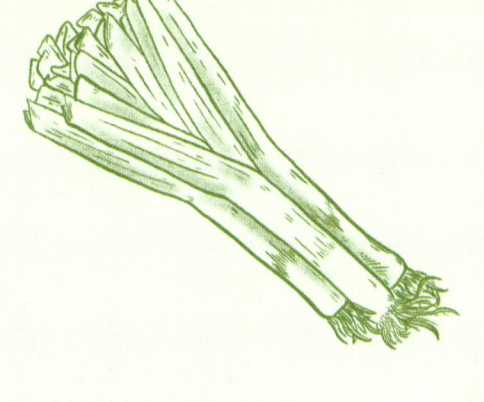

Using only the stalk of the leek, split down the middle lengthwise and sear with a little oil on the plancha, press with a small cast iron. Flip and repeat.

It should be soft and have a good amount of char to it. Chop into medium-sized pieces that will blend easier. Place on small sheet tray and allow to cool in the walk-in.

Once cool, add all the ingredients except the oil and xanthan gum in a blender cup and blend on high until the vegetables have broken down then slowly stream in the oil

Once all of the oil has been emulsified, slowly add the xanthan gum. Pass through chinois to remove any veg matter. Adjust seasoning if needed and store for up to two days.

MARINATED BEETS, MASA CHEESE CURDS & BLACK BEAN MOLE

ODD DUCK

For this fun, unexpected beet dish inspired by Mexico, we make our masa in-house because of its versatility, which goes far beyond tortillas. The beets are marinated in the cumin vinaigrette ahead of time. Put on gloves to fry the curds. Remember to let the extra batter drip off your fingers before sprinkling the coated curds into the fryer.

CUMIN VINAIGRETTE

2 ea.	morita chiles	.25 c	tequila
1 ea.	pasilla chile	1 pt	grapeseed oil
1 ea.	guajillo chile	1 tsp	xanthan gum
1 qt	rice wine vinegar	TT	salt
1 c	toasted cumin		

De-seed the chiles and put in a pot with the vinegar. Bring vinegar chile mix to a simmer and shut off the heat. Let sit until chiles are soft. Move mix to a blender add the toasted cumin, tequila, xanthan gum and blend on medium speed for a minute. Turn to high speed and slowly add oil, season and cool.

MASA CHEESE CURD BATTER

970 g	egg white
200 g	baking soda
800 g	masa
50 g	sea salt
1300 g	cornstarch

Dissolve masa in the egg whites until there are no clumps. Sift in the corn starch and baking soda as you whisk. Add in salt. Make sure the cornstarch and baking powder are lump-free. Pour over the curds as needed. Taste and adjust as needed. Label and package.

BLACK BEAN MOLE

2 lb	black beans
5 ea.	arbol chiles
5 ea.	guajillo chiles
5 ea.	pasilla chiles
5 ea.	ancho chiles
5 ea.	morita chiles
1 ea.	white onion *quartered*
20 ea.	garlic
.5 c	almonds
.5 c	peanuts
1 c	sesame seeds
.5 c	pepitas
1 c	pecans
1 in.	Mexican cinnamon
5 ea.	black peppercorns
1 tbsp	cumin
2 ea.	bay leaves

> "WE MAKE OUR MASA IN-HOUSE BECAUSE OF ITS VERSATILITY, WHICH GOES FAR BEYOND TORTILLAS."

1 c	golden raisins
.5 lb	green tomatoes
1 ea.	banana
40 g	cilantro stem
2 g	thyme
2 g	oregano
.25 c	brown sugar
6 oz	dark chocolate
3 ea.	grilled tortillas
.25 c	chile oil
TT	salt
TT	red wine vinegar

De-seed all chiles (keep seeds), toast and hydrate with some hot water. Toast nuts and seeds to a nice dark brown. Toast cumin.

Thinly slice the sweet potato and char-grill with onion, green tomatoes, and garlic. Place everything in the pressure cooker and with enough water to cover. Cook for five minutes at high pressure and then 12 more minutes at normal pressure. Turn off and drop pressure altogether. Blend and strain mole. Season with salt, red wine vinegar and more chile oil to taste.

SHRIMP RADISH COCKTAIL

BARLEY SWINE

This dish is meant to mimic a classic shrimp cocktail in a glass. The sauce is made from fermented watermelon radish rather than ketchup. We wrap the shrimp with pickled radish to add texture and accentuate the radish. It is then dipped in the sauce, rested on the glass for ease of grabbing, and garnished with cilantro flowers and crispy beer batter bits.

PANTRY STAPLE
BOIL SPICE

90 g	mustard seed
30 g	coriander
25 g	allspice
25 g	dill seed
5 g	cloves
5 g	bay leaves
20 g	celery seed
30 g	cayenne
55 g	onion powder
20 g	garlic powder

Toast, blend, and strain. The yield is a quart.

POACHED SHRIMP. Use boil spice recipe. Heavily season water with 10% spice and 1.5% salt and one charred lime per gallon. Bring poaching liquid to a boil. Add shrimp. Stir until 75% cooked, then cool down in ice bath with just enough liquid to cover the shrimp. You can use the poaching liquid twice.

PICKLED DAIKON. Spiralize large purple daikon. Season with 1% salt. Press in 5% lime.

BEER BATTERED SESAME. Equal parts weight, raw sesame, beer batter, and more beer.

COCKTAIL SAUCE. Three parts radish kimchi, two parts rice wine vinegar, and one part sugar. Fish sauce to taste. Bring ingredients to a boil. Simmer four to five minutes. Blend on high with .3% xanthan gum and 1% fish sauce. Blend until smooth and pass through chinois.

REDFISH CEVICHE

ODD DUCK

One of our oldest dishes on the menu, this ceviche changes with the season but the concept stays the same. There's a lot of flavor with the fish mix alone and it is enhanced further with the seasonal curry puree. The redfish is filleted and skin removed, then lightly cured to firm the flesh and season. We dice it and portion it at two ounces each. Before serving, we toss the portions with equal parts relish, lime juice and toasted garlic oil to taste. The curry can be made with carrots, squash, or whatever you want. The dish is finished with chips, made from whatever potato is in season.

CEVICHE RELISH

1 qt	Castelvetrano olives
1 qt	roasted golden beets
1 c	red onion
1 c	cilantro stems

Drain and dry olives, and toss with a splash of grapeseed oil. In a perforated pan, grill olives, developing good color and grill marks. In a Robot Coupe, pulse olives three or four times, but do not overprocess. Peel and large dice the golden beets. Small dice the red and white onion. Mince cilantro stems and combine all ingredients well.

CILANTRO-LIME DRESSING

300 g	onions *cut into large pieces*	3 in.	ginger *peeled and sliced*
50 g	garlic *halved lengthwise*	.25 tsp	citric acid *two pinches*
1 pt	fennel juice	3 ea.	lime zest *Microplaned*
1 pt	cucumber juice		
1 c	orange juice	1 c	olive oil
.5 c	tequila	6 ea.	ice
3 ea.	cilantro bunches	2 g	xanthan gum
2 ea.	parsley bunches	TT	salt

Blanch onion and garlic in lightly salted water and then shock in ice water. Blanch onion and garlic in same water until they are translucent, and shock in the same ice water. Once onions, garlic, and herbs and cooled, remove from water and squeeze all the water out of them. Cut the bunches of herbs into smaller pieces to make it easier to blend and place in the blender. Place everything else in the blender and run on high for 45 seconds to a minute before adding oil to emulsify. Season with chile ferment liquid and vinegar to taste. Strain and put in an ice bath to chill for a good 25 minutes before putting away.

SWEET POTATO CURRY

75 g	garlic
75 g	ginger
3 g	ají amarillo
1000 g	sweet potatoes
700 g	coconut milk
15 g	lemongrass
2 ea.	kaffir lime
25 g	fish sauce
25 g	sea salt

Toast sliced garlic in grapeseed oil, add sliced ginger and sweat until softened. Add peeled and diced sweet potato, sea salt and sweat briefly with lid. Add coconut milk, bring to boil, and reduce to simmer. The starch in the sweet potatoes should thicken the liquid. Cook until the sweet potatoes are extremely soft and can be easily crushed with a spoon. Add lime leaves and lemongrass, cover to steep. Puree until extremely smooth, strain, and adjust with mushroom broth. Acidity in the dish will come from tiger's milk and spice from fresh serrano. Keep these things in mind when balancing the sauce.

Note: It's important to use sea salt, as it is a seafood dish.

ANTELOPE TATAKI, GREEN GARLIC MAYO & ROSEMARY CRACKERS

ODD DUCK

Nilgai antelope leg from Broken Arrow Ranch gets spiced with chile powder and quickly grilled, remaining raw in the middle. We dice and marinate it with pickled red cabbage, beef fat, sesame seeds, pumpkin seed and radish. Basically, this dish is like a meat ceviche.

GREEN GARLIC MAYO

200 g	green garlic *trimmed & charred*
10 g	red wine vinegar
50 g	mustard
25 g	garlic *Microplaned*
6 ea.	egg yolks
600 g	green garlic oil
TT	salt

Char the green garlic and then let cool all the way down. Slice garlic thin like you would green onions. Put green garlic and yolks in Robot Coupe and mix for about 20 seconds. Make mayo, season and taste.

ROSEMARY CRACKERS

1200 g	AP flour
10 g	salt
15 g	sugar
480 g	water *filtered room temp*
3 ea.	eggs
180 g	butter *melted*
3 g	instant yeast
3 c	rosemary *chopped*
1 ea.	bottle olive oil
1 c	Maldon salt

Mix all ingredients in a stand mixer with the dough hook attachment for three minutes on speed one at first and then two minutes on speed two. Loosely wrap in plastic wrap and rest overnight in the cooler. Cracker dough needs to rest for at least one hour before rolling out.

    Cracker dough gets split into four equal balls. Each ball gets rolled-out to the right thickness that's going to fit into the pasta machine. The dough gets rolled out with the pasta machine to setting number five. Lightly spray the rolled out crackers with water. Evenly distribute rosemary on the sprayed dough. Be sure to get even coverage for every step. Next, drizzle olive oil over the dough followed with salt and fresh cracked black pepper. Crush the Maldon salt between your fingers as you season. Finally, take a full sheet of parchment and lay it over sheet trays with built crackers. Press down lightly to ensure everything stays on the cracker. Bake in a 325-degree oven, turning every six minutes until golden-brown. Cool and store.

ROAST BEEF SANDWICH, PICKLED CARROT & KIMCHI

ODD DUCK

Ranger Cattle produces beautiful tri-tip from their Wagyu, which we smoke and then slice cold. The ciabatta is one of my favorite offerings from Sour Duck Market. The sandwich build is tamarind mayo, chopped seasonal kimchi (mostly radish and greens), sliced beef, pickled carrots, and herbs.

DANNY'S KIMCHI PASTE

300 g	ginger
225 g	garlic
2 ea.	green onion bunches
25 g	ferment mash
5 g	red pepper flake
1 c	white sugar
50 g	chipotle power
40 g	sweet paprika
250 g	previous ferment liquid from greens

Peel ginger and cut into small pieces that will blend well in the Robot Coupe. Wash green onions and cut into small pieces. Process everything in batches. It should be a chunky paste with the consistency of a salsa.

Salt quantity should be 2.5% of vegetable weight. Wash and dry all vegetables thoroughly. Take the total weight of the vegetables and multiply that number by .025 and that will give you the weight of the salt needed to toss the vegetables in. Add the kimchi paste and mix thoroughly. Allow to sit for 10 minutes, then store in a container with bubble lid for four days.

CIABATTA PULLMAN LOAF

%	INGREDIENT	6 LOAVES	8 LOAVES	10 LOAVES
96.00	water	4237	5649	7061
70.00	bread flour	3089	4119	5149
30.00	semolina	1324	1765	2207
1.00	red yeast	44	59	74
1.50	salt	66	88	110
198.50		8760	11680	14600

Scale water and flours into mixing bowl, scale salt and yeast and set aside.

1st speed. 5-min.

Autolyse 15 to 20-min.

1st speed. 5-min. Sprinkle in and incorporate salt and yeast.

Bulk ferment 15-min., divide, and shape into pullman.

Proof in box until near the top.

PRODUCT	SCALING	BAKING
pullman loaf	1400	--
torta	120	One pullman batch divided into 12 squares

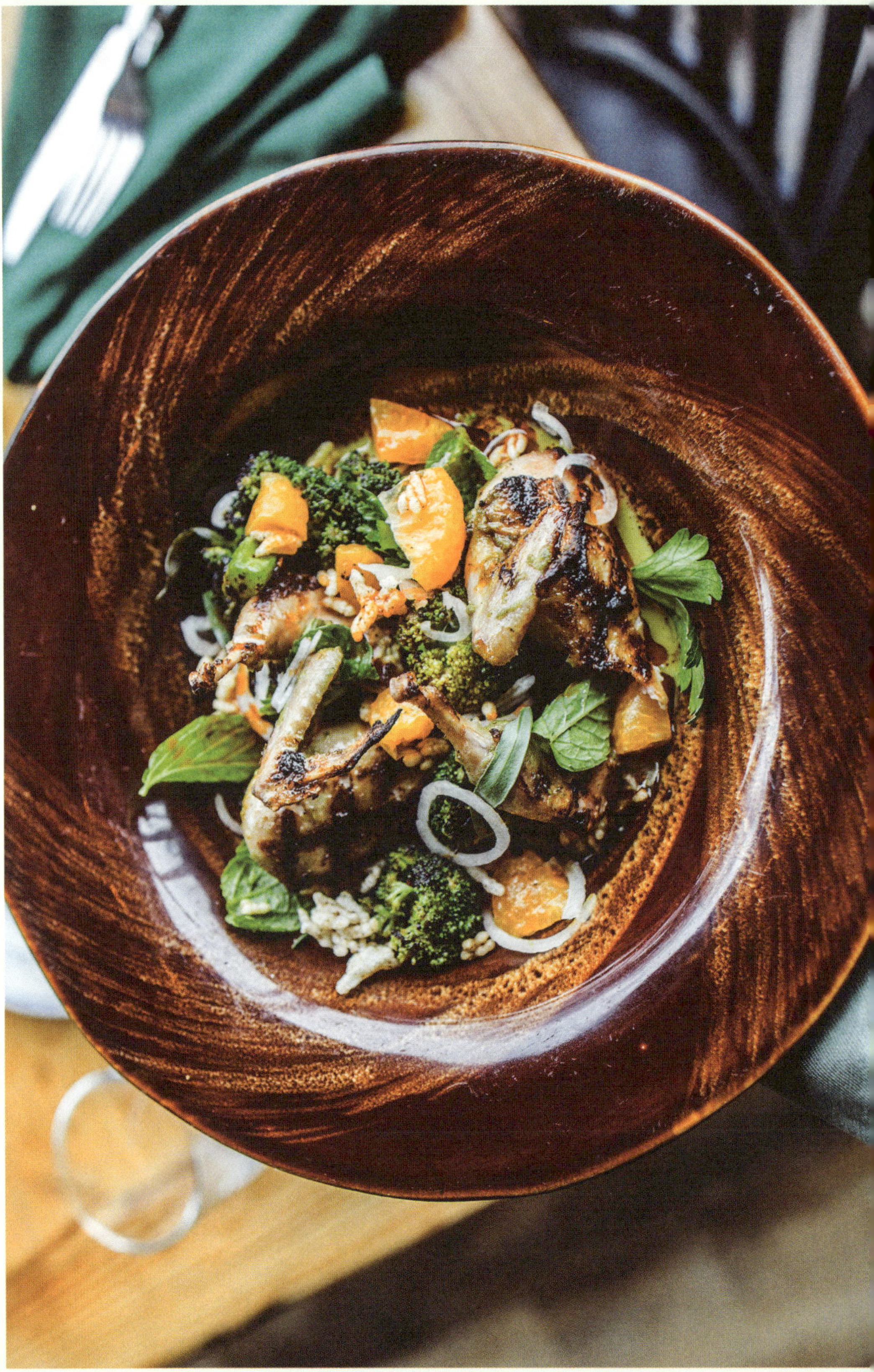

GRILLED QUAIL, GREEN GARLIC BISQUE & SNAP PEAS

ODD DUCK

Our quail is sourced from Diamond H Ranch, a sister company of Broken Arrow. For this recipe, the bird is brined and marinated with green garlic and ginger and then cooked on our wood-burning grill. It is served over a bisque with lots of herbs, grilled snap peas tossed in chile oil, and finished with puffed rice, and ras el hanout—a North African spice blend.

GREEN GARLIC BISQUE

30 ea.	green garlic stalks and white bulbs
1330 g	heavy cream
1 qt	tarragon
227g	butter
4 qt	pork stock
2 ea.	bay leaf
4 qt	spinach

Slice the green garlic stalks and white garlic bulbs separately, then sweat the white garlic with the butter until translucent. Add the cream and reduce for 10 minutes. Add the green garlic, bay leaf, and stock and reduce for another 20 minutes. Meanwhile, blanch the tarragon and spinach and then cool. Remove the bay leaf, then work in batches blending the blanched veggies, strain through a chinois and season with salt and pepper.

PANTRY STAPLE

RAS EL HANOUT

120 g	black pepper
88 g	coriander
22 g	cinnamon
28 g	cloves
60 g	cumin
18 g	juniper
1 ea.	nutmeg
15 g	cayenne

Lightly toast the spices, except for the cayenne, until fragrant. Let cool, blend, and pass through a china cap. You will have to blend it and strain it a few times to get the best yield. Mix with the cayenne.

STRAWBERRY BAKED GOODS

SOUR DUCK MARKET

Ripe strawberries simply sliced and arranged over this cake are awesome. The white chocolate and lemon pair nicely with the berries.

BROWN BUTTER CAKE

110 g	butter *tempered*
80 g	brown butter *tempered*
500 g	sugar
120 g	brown sugar
6 ea.	eggs *tempered*
220 g	buttermilk *tempered*
130 g	grapeseed oil
4 g	vanilla
370 g	AP flour
8 g	baking powder
8 g	salt

Sift dry ingredients together. Cream butters and sugars together using a stand mixer and paddle attachment. Add eggs one at a time on medium speed. Mix together buttermilk, oil, vanilla and slowly stream down side of bowl. Continue whipping mixture on medium high until almost doubled in volume.

Add in dry ingredients towards the end on low speed. Finish folding with spatula and make sure everything is evenly distributed.

Measure 750 grams of batter into half sheet pans and bake five minutes, rotate, and bake for five more minutes at 325 degrees, or until lightly browned.

LEMON CURD

258 g	lemon juice		168 g	butter
4 ea.	yolks		pinch	salt
4 ea.	eggs		pinch	vanilla
168 g	sugar		2 ea.	gelatin sheets

Melt butter, lemon juice, sugar, salt, and vanilla together. Combine eggs in separate bowl. When mixture boils, turn off heat and temper into eggs. Put back mixture back in pot and cook until thickened. Bloom gelatin. Before mixture thickens too much, whisk in gelatin until dissolved. Strain through a chinois and let cool.

WHITE CHOCOLATE GANACHE

350 g	white chocolate
225 g	heavy cream
pinch	salt
pinch	vanilla paste
200 g	soft whipped cream
3 ea.	gelatin sheets

Bloom gelatin. Bring heavy cream, vanilla, and salt to boil. Whisk in gelatin and immediately pour over white chocolate and mix to fully incorporate. Whisk together with soft whipped cream once cooled.

Line half sheet tray with parchment and place first sponge in cake ring. Cover with four cups of curd. Move pan around to distribute evenly and use a spatula if needed. If curd is not cooled completely, it will spread more easily. Chill.

Place second sponge over curd. Pour white chocolate ganache over sponge and freeze.

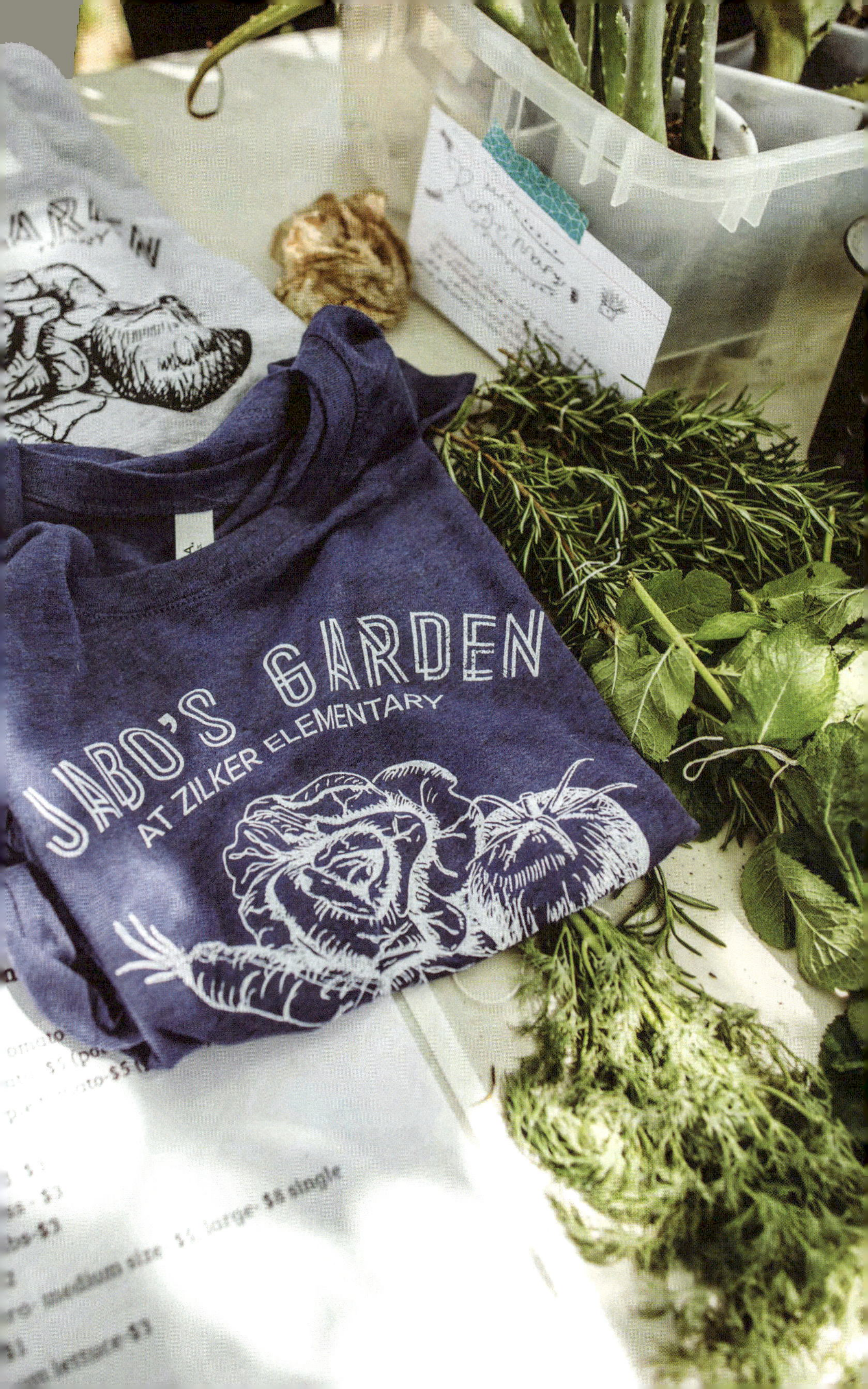
JABO'S GARDEN
AT ZILKER ELEMENTARY

Mother's Little HELPERS

IT'S A SUNNY SPRING AFTERNOON, AND ZILKER ELEMENTARY IS A FLURRY OF ENERGY—BUT IT'S NOT RECESS TIME.

A CROWD OF PARENTS AND NEIGHBORS circulate from table to table, where kids are selling bountiful bunches of herbs and greens from their community garden. Another area is filled with cups of aloe vera, and junior gardeners demonstrate how the plant can be cut open and used topically. Other students pass out homemade lemonade enhanced with basil, lavender or mint, and sell hand-made herbal soap and Jabo's Garden t-shirts.

Recipe Ideas!
Jabo's Edible & Instructional Gar
PLEASE
No dogs allowed
No picking plants
For Zilker Elementary school use only

Nearly a decade ago, Jerry "Jabo" Dean, a retired University of Texas music professor, began volunteering his time to garden with his grandson's Zilker Elementary kindergarten class, and he's been gardening with every kindergarten class ever since. In 2014, the chef-owners of Odd Duck approached the school and offered to help expand the program and pass along their passion for food and sustainability to a new generation. Jabo's Garden was born and has been thriving ever since.

> "THERE ARE SURELY SOME FUTURE CHEFS SPROUTING IN SOUTH AUSTIN."

Each year, Odd Duck donates to help Zilker with the upkeep and infrastructure of the garden. One hundred percent of the proceeds from the annual Odd Duck anniversary party and auction go toward Jabo's and sometimes a portion of sales from a particular dish will help fund the garden as well. This year, Odd Duck baked cookies to sell and Bryce was spotted buying produce from the kids to use in the restaurant.

Nearby, postcards were pinned to the garden fence; each one scrawled with handwritten recipes utilizing the season's bounty. The fence included tasty dishes like sweet and spicy Swiss chard, rosemary and Parmesan popcorn, and mango mint salad, to name a few.

This program might be cultivating more than just the land, because there are surely some future chefs sprouting in South Austin.

TOP
Zilker Elementary students Emily, Madeline, Marley, Siena, and Ella show off their harvest of herbs and aloe vera.

BOTTOM
Bryce checks out some of the students' recipes on the idea fence.

FROM THE FARM

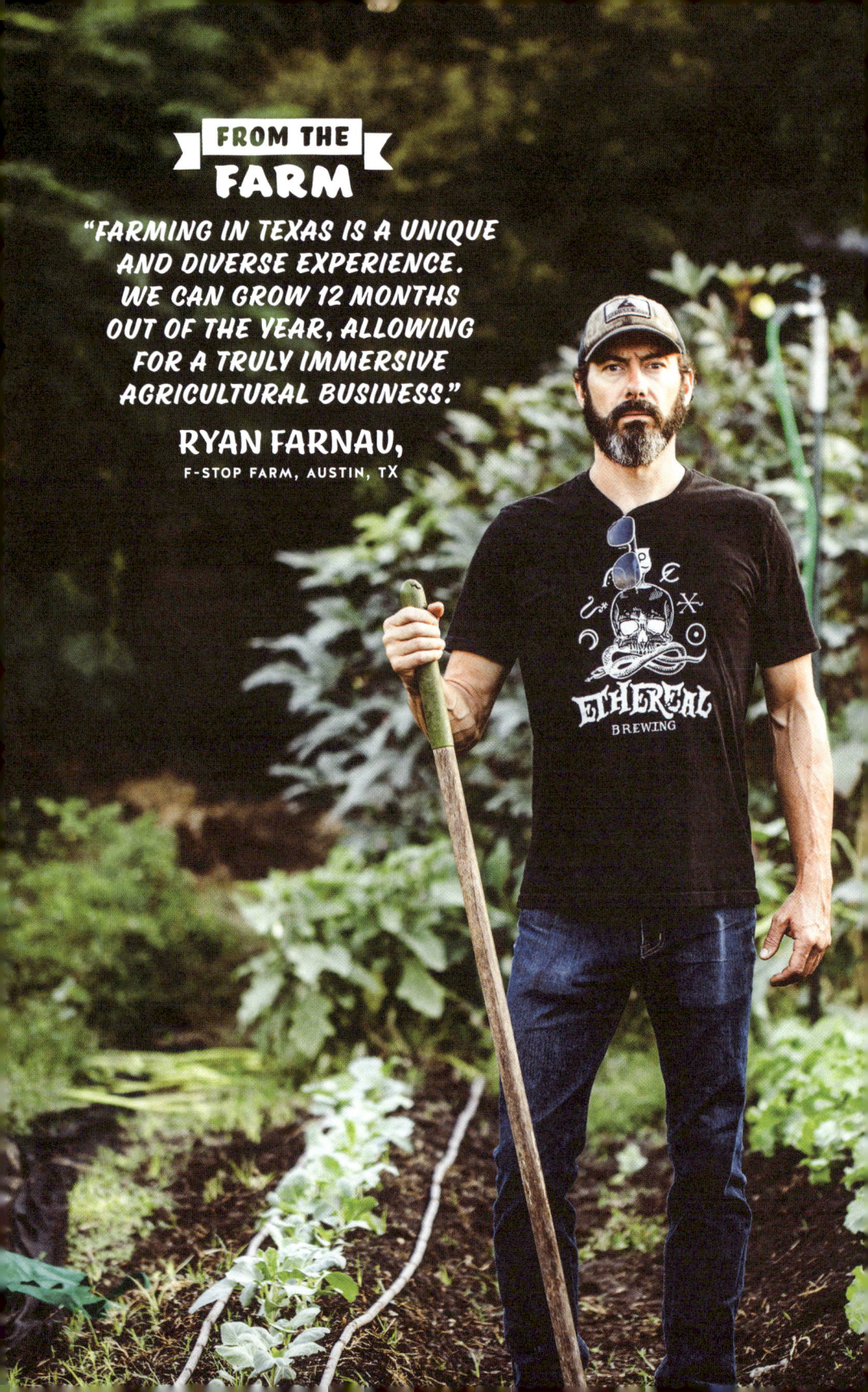

"FARMING IN TEXAS IS A UNIQUE AND DIVERSE EXPERIENCE. WE CAN GROW 12 MONTHS OUT OF THE YEAR, ALLOWING FOR A TRULY IMMERSIVE AGRICULTURAL BUSINESS."

RYAN FARNAU,
F-STOP FARM, AUSTIN, TX

RECIPES FOR SUMMER

MAY–OCTOBER

HOTTER THAN HADES

FUCK GLOBAL WARMING.
THIS TRIPLE DIGIT TORTURE
GETS HARDER EACH YEAR.

THERE'S NO DENYING that Summer in central Texas is brutal. But it's also an exciting time when we see the most extensive variety of fruit and produce. Farmers make the most of their income for the year in these months, so the pressure is on, and the work is non-stop. Summer ingredients like corn, green beans, and tomatoes begin to appear in early June, phase out when it gets too hot, and reappear again at the end of the season when the heat starts to subside. July and August bring okra, melon, eggplant and a ton of different types of peppers, ranging from sweet to hot. We preserve these to make sure we have fermented peppers all year round. There's also a Summer harvest of potatoes including Kennebecs, Yukons, and Russets, which are great for chips and frying. Next time you find yourself complaining about the Texas heat, get out to the market, and see what your local farmers have been cultivating under that relentless sun.

CRAB PIMENTO, SHISHITO ONION DIP & GRILLED POTATOES

ODD DUCK

You can mix anything into this pimento recipe, and it instantly tastes even more fantastic! This version features blue crab meat from the Gulf of Mexico, which works nicely with the grilled potatoes and shishito onion dip.

CRAB PIMENTO CHEESE

1 qt	green chile mayo
20 ea.	soft-scrambled eggs
2 qt	cheddar
1.5 qt	Oaxaca cheese
1 c	oregano *finely chopped*
1 c	minced onion
.5 c	pickled jalapeño liquid
25 turns	black pepper
.25 c	spicy chile ferment
.5 c	fresh jalapeño
25 g	salt
2 ea.	garlic *Microplaned*

Blend the eggs with a splash of cream. Soft scramble in a pot by starting on mid-high heat, but flames should not climb the sides of the pan. Whisk them bitches when they first begin to coagulate. Turn down the heat to low and whisk until soft scrambled. Cool the eggs on a half sheet tray lined with parchment. For the mayo, whisk together four egg yolks, one egg, and one tbsp of Dijon. Treat chile oil like regular oil to make the mayo.

Note: you may need to cut the oil with grapeseed if it is too spicy. Once the eggs are cool, mix everything together in a large bowl and season with white distilled vinegar and salt if needed.

RECIPES FOR SUMMER

SHISHITO ONION DIP

1725 g	sour cream
250 g	chives
700 g	shishito peppers
200 g	garlic confit and oil
90 g	white balsamic vinegar
565 g	cream
48 g	salt
2 g	locust bean gum
1 g	xanthan gum

Wash all shishitos and green onion. Take the tops off of the shishitos. Save scrap for future chile oil.

In an eight quart pot weigh out the cream, sour cream, garlic confit and oil, white balsamic and half of the shishitos. Set aside.

In a perforated pan over a raging fire, char remaining shishitos. Add charred shishitos to everything else and bring up to 160 degrees. shut off heat and allow to steep for about 20 minutes. In batches while still hot, blend together chives, dairy, shishitos, grilled onions, garlic confit (oil and all) and sprinkles of both locust bean gum and xanthan gum. The two gums help emulsify the oil into the dairy and keeps it from breaking. This means that you're going to want some in every blender-full that you blend. Strain through a chinois once totally blended, season, and package.

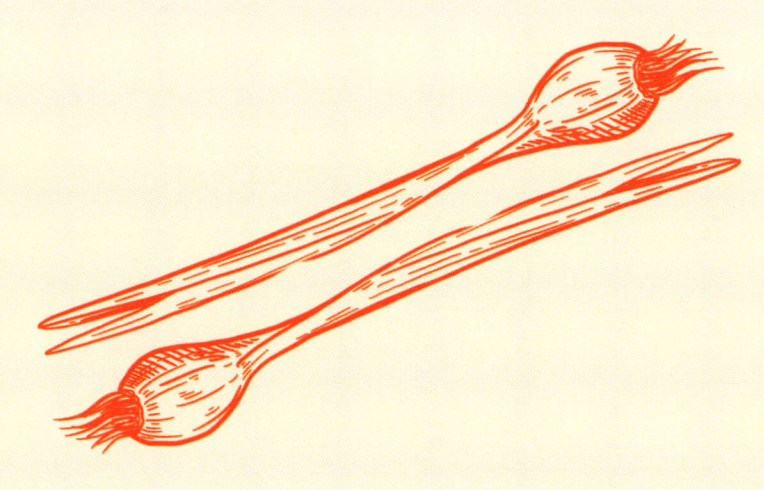

CHARRED GREEN BEANS MARINATED WITH TARE & TOGARASHI

SOUR DUCK MARKET

After you make the tare, this is a simple dish. The green beans are charred on the flat top then cooled down, tossed in the tare sauce, and finished with the Sour Duck Market togarashi.

TARE

680 g	onion *sliced*
200 g	celery *sliced*
2 ea.	charred onion
320 g	garlic
400 g	ginger
1000 g	sugar
4 g	star anise
4 g	all spice
1 g	cloves
6 g	Vietnamese cinnamon
12 g	orange peel
365 g	mushroom trim or liquid
4000 g	fish stock

In a rondeau, char all vegetables until dark and almost burnt. Turn off heat, add sugar, and make a caramel. Crack with fish stock and add everything else. Reduce to simmer for one and a half hours. Blend then strain and steep lemongrass in mixture while cooling.

TOGARASHI

300 g	blanched almonds
300 g	pepitas
200 g	hemp seed
200 g	sunflower seeds
200 g	sesame seeds
200 g	poppy seeds
25 g	orange zest
25 g	dried ginger
62 g	black pepper
45 g	arbol powder

Zest orange, and let dry out. Toast the black pepper and arbols for one minute and then grind them into a powder and sift. Toast almonds and pepitas together but toast the sunflower seeds separately. Toast the rest of the seeds together and then mix everything together.

THE ODD DUCK ALMANAC

PIG HEAD TERRINE, HOT SAUCE, FIG, PEARS & CRACKERS

ODD DUCK

We love pork—especially face meat! It is the epitome of what the animal has to offer: pure pork flavor from all the bone and cartilage. The gelatinous nature of the head meat adds a sticky, nasty finger-licking goodness. The terrine is simply a boiled pig's head, shredded with skin and all, then set into a loaf that is sliced and served slightly warm. The hot sauce brings heat and brightness, and the late-Summer fruit balances the dish out with a subtle sweetness. We serve this with our rosemary crackers (pg. 75).

FRESNO HOT SAUCE

1000 g	Fresno ferment
4000 g	distilled vinegar
50 g	salt
30 g	garlic raw
20 g	xanthan gum

Blend all ingredients together, in batches. Shear xanthan gum into two of the batches. Mix all blended batches together. Bottle, label, and store.

SHIITAKE DUMPLINGS WITH SCRAMBLED EGG & GRILLED ZUCCHINI

BARLEY SWINE

At Barley Swine, this dish has been on our a la carte menu since we moved to the Burnet Road location. Inspired by soup dumplings, we fill cooked pasta with a savory soup mixture that creates a surprising explosion in your mouth. The scrambled egg adds richness to the bright and flavorful filling, and the garnishes change with the season.

SHIITAKE CHIP. Fry sliced shiitake in clarified butter until golden, season with sea salt and dehydrate.

SOFT SCRAMBLED EGG
- 900 g   eggs
- 90 g   cream
- 10 g   salt

Blend and circulate at 72 degrees until scrambled.

PASTA FILLING
- 350 g   butter
- 120 g   grapeseed oil
- 1200 g   shiitakes *processed*
- 200g   shallots *sliced*
- 160 g   garlic *sliced*
- 80 g   ginger *sliced*
- 200 g   sake
- 250 g   tamarind
- 1400 g   mushroom stock
- 750 g   fermented shiitakes
- 250 g   premium white soy sauce
- 750 g   rice wine vinegar

Fry shiitakes in oil until golden. Add shallot, garlic, ginger and sweat. Deglaze with sake and tamari, reduce until almost dry. Add ferment and stock and bring to simmer. Cover with plastic and let sit for 30 minutes. Add soy and vinegar then puree. Then blend in to finish:

350 g butter / 1600 g puree
1 sheet bloomed gelatin / 50 g puree

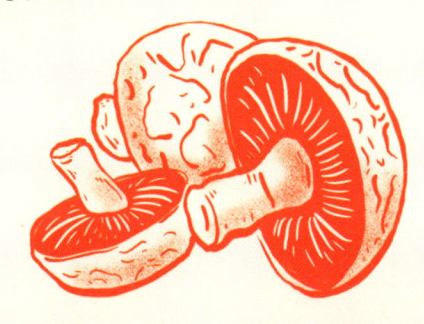

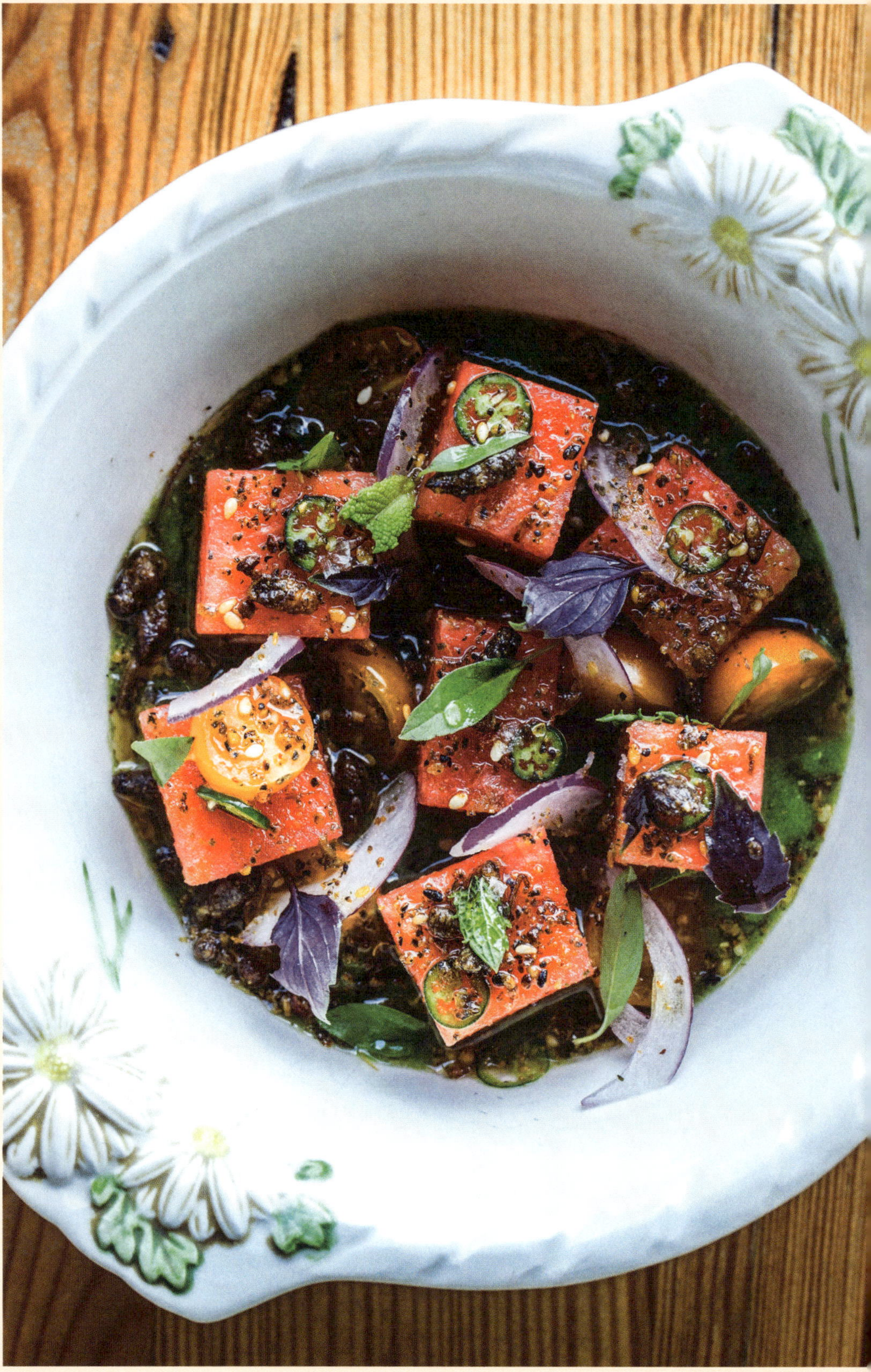

MARINATED MELONS

ODD DUCK

Chile oil is the go to for garnishing at the pass. Before it leaves the kitchen, most dishes likely get a couple of drops of this oil to add color and a touch of spice. These marinated melons incorporate the byproduct from making the oil. Usually, we'll top this dish off with goat feta and pumpkin seeds. We've even tried adding cricket togarashi, and crispy pig ears.

MELON CHILE MARINADE

400 g	chile paste *from chile oil*
60 g	salt
80 g	honey
8 g	hot sauce
296 g	red wine vinegar

Whisk everything together until smooth.

PANTRY STAPLE

CHILE OIL

400 g	whole garlic
500 g	grapeseed oil
35 ea.	guajillo
10 ea.	arbol
4 ea.	morita
4 ea.	pasilla
3000 g	grapeseed oil
50 g	paprika

Toast garlic in grapeseed until golden-brown. Once toasty, add grapeseed oil and chiles. Bring back up to 180 degrees. Finish with paprika and plastic wrap for 30 minutes. Blend like crazy. Strain in fryer filter. Package and label.

FRIED QUAIL, CREAMED CORN & PEACH HOT SAUCE

ODD DUCK

As good as the grilled quail can be, well guess what . . . fried quail ain't bad either! This one was garnished with blistered shishitos and grilled mushrooms to add some earthiness.

QUAIL. Brine the quail for half a day before soaking it in buttermilk overnight. Before serving, toss quail in a **SEEDED DREDGE** and lay it out in the fridge to allow the flour mixture to adhere.

MAMA SAID

Waste not, want not. Use the same **SEEDED DREDGE** from the fried fish head recipe on page 40. A flour and cornmeal mix will also make do in a pinch.

Fry at 350 degrees until golden-brown. Quail should still be pink in the middle when cut in half. Check for 130 internal temp.

PEACH HOT SAUCE

2565 g	peaches *cleaned*
675 g	red wine vinegar
335 g	sugar
5 g	arbol chiles *deseeded*
5 g	morita chiles *deseeded*
1.5 g	agar agar

Cut peaches into medium dice and put all ingredients in a pot. Bring to a boil and then turn heat down to medium. Simmer mixture until peaches are soft. Blend everything together and strain. Season with salt to taste. Place in an ice bath to cool.

CREAMED CORN

10 lb	corn
750 g	white onions *thinly sliced*
62 g	garlic *minced*
8 g	turmeric
1 lb	butter
375 g	Scamorza cheese
1 gal	heavy cream
.5 gal	coconut milk
TT	salt and pepper

Melt butter in a rondeau until foaming. Add onions, garlic and sauté until they are lightly brown. Add corn, a pinch of salt and continue to sauté for a few minutes while stirring the bottom. Add creams, turmeric and reduce until the corn is tender. Pull off the fire and while the mixture is still hot, blend half of the corn mixture with the Scamorza cheese. You want to do this in stages to help dissolve the cheese, and it does not need to be perfectly smooth. Add blended mixture back into the pot with the rest of the corn, season and place in an ice bath to cool.

RECIPES FOR SUMMER

SUMMER BURGER WITH FRIED OKRA

ODD DUCK

We are very proud of our Odd Duck burger. When we first opened, I was very much against having a burger on the menu. I was trying to be different and not offer something that people can get almost anywhere else. But to be honest, lunch business wasn't all that great at Odd Duck, and eventually, we decided, fuck it, we'll do a burger and make it bad ass. This recipe changes with the seasons and sometimes at the whim of the kitchen. All of our bread is made at Sour Duck Market and brought over daily.

The burger is topped with a piece of fried okra which adds a great crunch! Okra is an ingredient that grows really well in Texas and we've seen some great varieties over the years. I love okra no matter how it's prepared. It has great flavor and I seem to be one of the few who don't mind its texture. Regardless, okra is always best fried! We cut the okra in half and soak it in buttermilk. Then toss them in a flour and cornmeal mixture before frying.

We've worked with a variety of ranchers over the years for the beef we use in our burger. It's all about finding that right ratio of fat in the grind. Currently we use 44 Farms and Ranger Cattle Wagyu. The wood grill at Odd Duck gives our burger its distinctive smoky flavor. Right before it comes off the grill, we top it off with our **BEER CHEESE**.

BURGER BUNS

360 g	AP flour
8 g	yeast
40 g	sugar
7 g	salt
50 g	potato flour
45 g	butter
230 g	milk
50 g	egg

MAMA SAID

You'd a be damn fool not to use the **BEER CHEESE** recipe from page 25. A burger without cheese is sacrilege after all.

Eggs and milk on bottom, yeast and flour on top. Scale sugar, and butter, set aside. four minutes, speed one. Add sugar, salt, and yeast; speed one until incorporated. seven minutes, speed two. Scrape bowl, combine dough. Add butter on speed one. After development, mix until fully incorporated. Speed two for one minute after butter incorporation. Each bun weighs 120 grams.

HEIRLOOM TOMATO & PEACH SALAD WITH CHEVRE

ODD DUCK

One of my favorite ways to build a salad is to make a chevre spread that gets swiped on the plate underneath everything. It acts as an extra dressing and helps season everything, adding extra flavor. The addition of shishitos takes this dish to the next level.

SHISHITO PEPPER GOAT CHEESE

400 g	grilled shishitos	*de-stemmed, deseeded*
300 g	goat chevre	
300 g	goat feta	
100 g	chile vinegar	
100 g	chile oil or other tasty oil	

Paddle the cheeses and vinegar, then drizzle in oil. Fold in chopped peppers.

SUNNY DUCK EGG WITH GOAT SAUSAGE & BROWN RICE

ODD DUCK

This dish is Odd Duck's version of fried rice using Summer veggies like okra, young butternut squash, and green beans. The goat sausage is inspired by Chinese sausage that has a little sugar, and the nuoc cham adds salinity and umami flavors.

CHINESE GOAT SAUSAGE

10 lb	ground goat
5 lb	goat liver
5 lb	pork scrap
4 g	pink salt
60 g	salt
100 g	Chinese wine
40 g	Szechuan peppercorn
40 g	raw sugar
80 g	chipotle powder
10 g	five spice blend

Mix everything together and grind once. Place in the mixer with the paddle attachment and mix at speed one for five minutes. Portion into five bags and freeze.

NUOC CHAM

1 bottle	fish sauce
1 pt	lime juice
1 pt	raw sugar
1 pt	rice wine vinegar
100 g	cilantro stems *small rounds*
25 g	Thai chiles *thin rings, seeds OK*
30 g	lemongrass *minced*
2 ea.	garlic cloves *Microplane*

RECIPES FOR SUMMER

Measure all liquids, mix with sugar and whisk together until sugar is dissolved. Add the rest of the ingredients. If there isn't any lemongrass use lime zest instead and Thai chile can be replaced with chile mash ferment.

BROWN RICE

1350 g	rice
2460 g	water
120 g	olive oil
45 g	salt
63 g	red wine vinegar

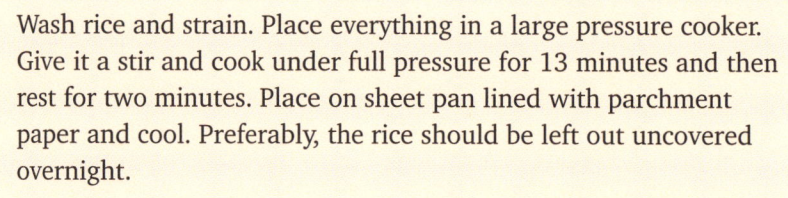

Wash rice and strain. Place everything in a large pressure cooker. Give it a stir and cook under full pressure for 13 minutes and then rest for two minutes. Place on sheet pan lined with parchment paper and cool. Preferably, the rice should be left out uncovered overnight.

SHISHITO SORBET WITH COCONUT YOGURT & MANGO CAKE CRUMBLE

ODD DUCK

Shishito peppers rock! They make everything better—even desserts. The pepper flavor in the sorbet pairs nicely with coconut and South Texas mangoes.

SORBET

4.5 ea.	shishito peppers
3800 g	lime juice
5500 g	sorbet base
20 g	ascorbic acid
35 g	citric acid
40 g	sea salt

Thoroughly clean the shishitos by cutting off the stems and scraping out the insides as much as possible. Using a Vitamix, add both lime juice and shishitos together and blend to a unified juice. Strain this juice through a chinois. Once all the shishitos have been juiced, add in all other ingredients and whisk. Adjust the seasoning if needed and spin.

SORBET BASE

1448 g	water
236 g	dextrose
1000 g	white sugar
54 g	stabilizer
1588 g	juice

Bring water to a simmer. Gather sugar, dextrose, and stabilizer into a Cambro and whisk dry ingredients together. Once water is up to temperature, stir in ingredients. Occasionally stir mixture for 15 minutes. Package and chill.

COCONUT YOGURT

1 can	coconut milk
450 g	organic sugar
15 g	agar agar
7 g	salt
5 ea.	lime zest
2 ea.	vanilla pod

Place a can of coconut milk into a stainless-steel pot with lime zest, sugar, and salt. Slowly bring up to a boil. Once at a boil, add in agar agar. Continuously stir for three minutes. After you have vigorously whisked, strain through a chinois, season and chill. This product will completely solidify. Once solid, blend in a Vitamix with a little bit of lime juice just to loosen up the product. Taste, quart up and label.

MANGO CAKE CRUMBLE

337 g	AP flour
14 g	baking powder
3 g	baking soda
3 g	salt
337 g	mango puree
75 g	coconut oil
150 g	sugar

Mix wet ingredients, except oil. Sift together all dry ingredients and mix well. Add wet ingredients into the dry and fold. Once incorporated, fold in warmed coconut oil. Spread cake batter evenly on a sheet tray and bake at 350 degrees for 30 minutes, or until done. Crumble the cakes once cooled and place crumble in dehydrator for at least 30 minutes.

MANGO PUREE

5 ea.	ripe mango
1.1%	xanthan gum
1 ea.	lime zest

Peel off all skin from the mango and remove it from the pit. Take the weight of the mango flesh and multiply it by .011. this will be the amount of xanthan gum you will need to thicken the puree. Add all ingredients to a Vitamix and blend until smooth. Taste, adjust, and package.

RECIPES FOR SUMMER

Farm-to-Table Partner

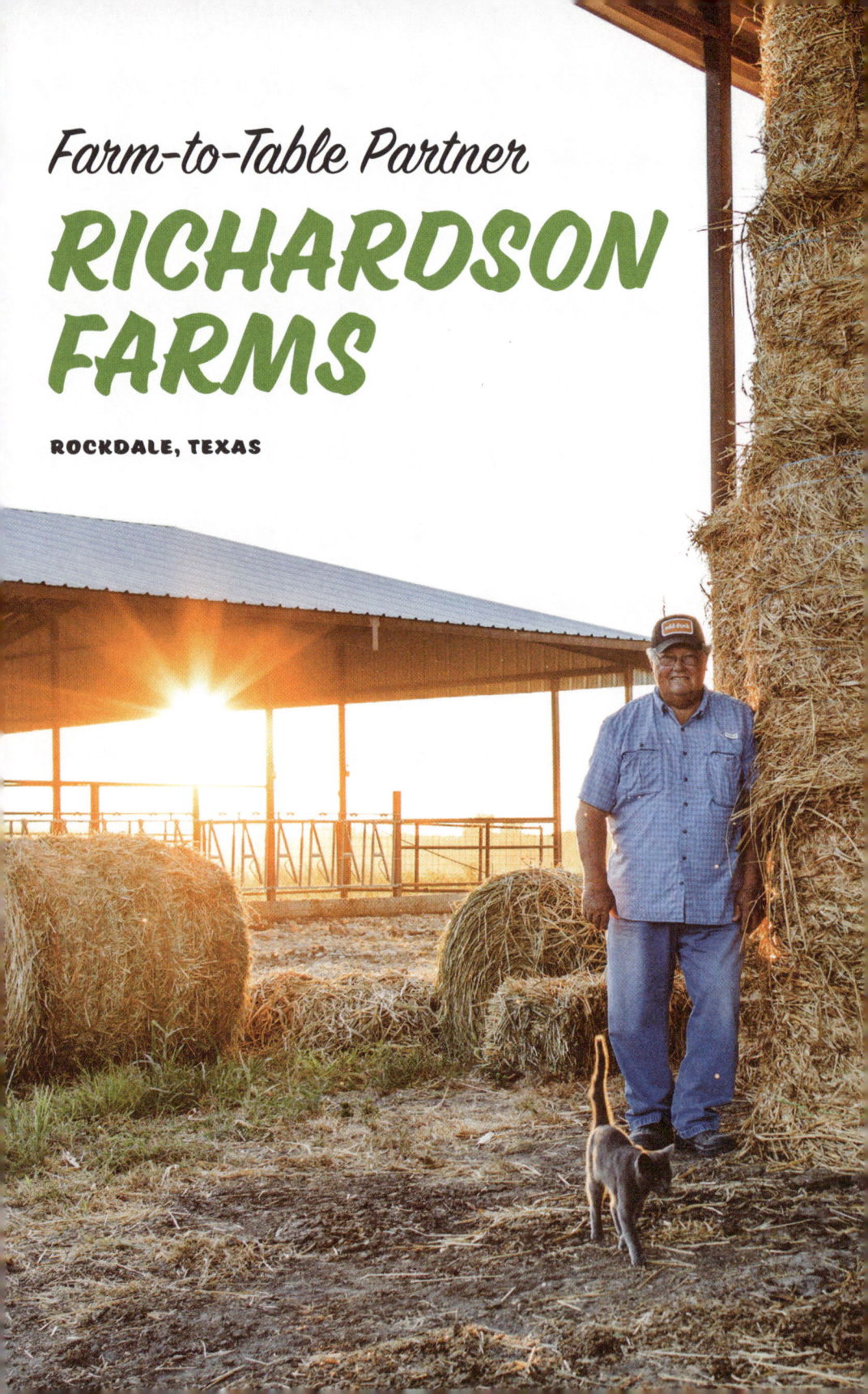

RICHARDSON FARMS

ROCKDALE, TEXAS

IF YOU FREQUENT THE BARTON CREEK FARMER'S MARKET, YOU'VE LIKELY MET JIM RICHARDSON, THE SMILING PROPRIETOR OF RICHARDSON FARMS.

JR: Most people meet me at the farmer's market while they're buying fresh, local food.

VM: That's precisely how Jim met Bryce and became the very first farmer to supply Odd Duck during the trailer days, selling him half a pig every week.

I told them, 'Take this protein and put your spin on it,' and the customers get all of the benefits. They get the local production, the humane care of the animals and the good, chemical-free products. These guys put their wrapper on it, and their culinary skills—and it just took off.

Jim grew up on his grandparents' small farm in North Texas, learning about how to care for animals and crops. He went on to study veterinary medicine at Texas A&M and worked as a veterinarian for 47 years.

I was always a person who liked working with animals. I'm a caretaker and a spokesman for animals and a welfare advocate. I wanted people to call on me, and trust me to go out to their farms and try to help solve their problems.

Jim always dreamed of having his own farm. In 2000, he and his wife made that dream come true by buying 200 acres of land in Rockdale, Texas, located about an hour northeast of Austin. He continued his veterinary work, commuting to Austin, for the next twelve years before finally retiring although he continues to consult by training vets in anesthesia and pain medicine his areas of expertise.

That gets me off the farm a day or two a month, he says with a chuckle.

Jim has become known for the Texas heirloom red wattle pigs he began raising in 2005.

The pigs are one of the main products we sell because there aren't a lot of people raising pigs in Texas. The only pigs that are really around here are called show pigs. They've got them so messed up with over-muscling, they push them hard with steroids to make them get big muscles, they can't move or walk, and that's what the judge awards.

As for chickens, he raises Freedom Rangers, a French heirloom breed, hatched in Lancaster, Pennsylvania.

It's a meaty chicken, but it's not as big or misshapen as the blackbirds bred in factory farms, where there are thousands of them in a building, and they don't walk at all. We raise our chickens outside, where they can graze, eat grass and bugs, and whatever else. Those big farms can get their birds ready in about seven weeks, and it takes us about twelve. So it's a slower, more time-involved process with more feed-involved, but we get a better product.

Jim also raises chickens for eggs, grass-fed Angus cows for beef and also milks Jersey cows on 25 separate acres. He opened a dairy three years ago, where he produces minimally processed milk and cheese. Standard pasteurization is 195 degrees, but they pasteurize at the minimum of 140 degrees to preserve the milk's protein and nutritional benefits.

> "WE'RE PROBABLY AS BIG AS WE'LL EVER GET AND THAT'S FINE BY ME."

There's a lot of people that now realize raw milk has merit, but they have to come all the way out here to buy it. I wish it wasn't that way, because it's so inconvenient for people. I think it's a lobbying effort by the big milk companies to hold a lid on the market. 99% of raw milk is produced by small farms, who also tend to take better care of their animals. They're not corporate factories pushing the animals as they do on the big farms, where all they care about is the money.

Though he can't legally sell raw milk at the market, he maintains a steady stream of customers who drive out to his farm to buy bottles on site. These type of consumers, who understand and appreciate the care put into his products, are the bread and butter of Jim's business. He's seen the most success with chef-owned restaurants like Odd Duck, Barley Swine, Jack Allen's Kitchen and Suerte.

People call me trying to compare the pricing they get from Sysco or Ben E. Keith or US Foods, and it's just not the same product or production environment. When you're getting the product from a supplier that has a million cattle, and they're working on a huge economy of scale, they can produce it cheaper than I can. I love to work with the small guys that are into what we're doing. We're probably as big as we'll ever get and that's fine by me.

Jim's very small staff consists of his wife who handles accounting, his brother who pasteurizes the milk, his cousin who grew up on the same farm with him, a retired local ("He's 66, and had a quadruple bypass, but he grew up working, and he's not satisfied sitting at home on the porch. You can't slow him down!" says Richardson) and another local woman who handles the cow milking.

I find that women tend to be more caring and well oriented toward hygiene— and way better at nurturing. We're milking these cows and bottling the milk, and these people are taking it home to their kids. It's got to be extra special and, to do that, you've got to have all the steps done perfectly.

When Jim first started his farm, he primarily grew grass, hay, and alfalfa to serve as feed for his animals. Now he's producing a variety of heirloom grains like non-GMO Bloody Butcher corn, heirloom hard red Winter wheat, old white African sorghum— and whatever else the chefs he works with might request.

> **"I TELL YOUNG FARMERS THEY NEED TO FIND SOME GOOD PEOPLE IN THE CULINARY WORLD AND GROW WHAT THOSE FOLKS WANT TO USE IN THEIR KITCHENS."**

I love to work with chefs. They teach me a lot of things, and I can help grow what they want. I tell young farmers they need to find some good people in the culinary world and grow what those folks want to use in their kitchens. It's not that hard! Different from Walmart because Walmart doesn't have your best interest at heart. You've got to have someone willing to play ball with you.

He recalls a time when a local chain restaurant decided to drop their account after their large order was already processed and loaded on the truck. Richardson saw Bryce's dad Jack at the farmer's market and told him what had happened. Rather than see the product go to waste, Jack bought it all on the spot and said he'd have his chefs create specials at his restaurants until it was gone.

And that's the kind of people we like to deal with, the kind that understand and are willing to collaborate. I can't say enough good about Jack, his wife Luann, Bryce and Dylan. The whole group are fine folks.

Jim has worked with up to 75 restaurants over the years and he's still continually garnering interest from new chefs.

We grew up growing grain for my grandfather, so we didn't know about the foodie craze—and when we came here, we got lucky and hit it at just the right time. The culinary scene was exploding in certain areas of the country, especially in Austin. There aren't any others in Texas better than Austin, in my opinion. Austin has the right people, and they've got the attitudes and talent that help keep it weird!

FROM THE FARM

"MY PRIMARY JOB IS EDUCATING CONSUMERS ON THEIR CHOICES BECAUSE THE MORE THEY KNOW, THE BETTER THEY CAN DO FOR THEMSELVES AND THEIR COMMUNITIES."

JONAS JONES,
GRAY GARDENS, BUDA, TX

RECIPES FOR AUTUMN

NOVEMBER–DECEMBER

THE SUPERIOR SEASON

IT'S SAFE TO COME OUT
AND DRINK AROUND THE BONFIRE.
AUSTIN IS THE BEST!

IN THE FALL, the succession of crops is like Spring in reverse. And since everything is already planted and weeded, it's pretty much all harvesting, all the time. As the heat eases up, a lot of the Summer produce starts to disappear, and there is often a period when the crisp weather vegetables haven't quite started to hit. This really puts a limit on the ingredients we have to work with and forces us to get even more creative. Then we begin to see more root vegetables like carrots and beets come in, plus apples, fennel, and pecans.

Interestingly enough, sweet potatoes and Winter squash like butternut, acorn, and kabocha are actually a late-Summer thing here, but many farmers hold onto them for Fall since so many people associate these ingredients with Thanksgiving. When broccoli, cauliflower, and kale begin to appear, we get really excited again for the wave of cool weather greens to start again. Kind of like breaking out your favorite sweater after it's been tucked away in storage all year long.

SMOKED FISH SALAD, TOSTADA, APPLE & FENNEL

ODD DUCK

Putting a tostada on the menu is almost too easy. With a crunchy corn chip as the base, it can elevate even a simple fish salad. We've been nixtamalizing corn at Odd Duck for a few years. Most of the corn comes from Richardson Farms, but Barton Springs Mill also has some great sources. There are many varieties of corn ranging in colors.

Redfish leftover from tacos or ceviche typically gets smoked. We pick and shred the fish then mix it with mayo and add garnishes like celery, dill, and onion. We sometimes go more regional by adding cilantro and chipotle. Raw apple and fennel give this satisfying snack a fresh and bright finish.

NIXTAMAL

1500 g	water
1 lb	dried corn
12 g	calcium oxide

If you are cooking less than six pounds of corn, up the water percentage to 2000 grams per pound of corn. Rinse the corn well. Cover the corn with the water, reserving a small amount to dissolve the calcium oxide. Bring the water up to a simmer, stir well and pour into the corn/water mixture. Bring to a simmer, covered, then drop to a light simmer and cook for about one and a half hours. This cook time is only a loose guideline, as the time will depend on how much corn you are using and the pot. Make sure the water is not at too hot or it will evaporate and give the corn a chemical taste. Make sure to stir often. This is very important.

When the corn is tender and about 70% cooked, pull off the heat, pour into a Cambro and adjust the water level to account for the evaporation. Ratio is as follows: one pound of dry corn is three cups. 1500 grams of water is seven cups. Do the math and adjust accordingly.

6.5 lb	masa yields 75 tortillas
4 lb	dry corn yields 80 tortillas

Once tortillas are pressed, cook on the flat top thoroughly, landing them on a sheet tray once finished. When tortillas are cooked they can be cut and fried in a 300-degree fryer and seasoned with sea salt when they come out.

SWEET POTATO, ONION CAPER JAM, JALAPEÑO CHEVRE & PECAN COOKIE

ODD DUCK

These sweet potatoes are roasted in butter in the wood oven and tossed with an onion caper jam. We use the chevre spread technique to go underneath everything.

ONION CAPER JAM

10 lb	onion *small diced*
32 oz	currants
64 oz	apple cider vinegar
32 oz	raw sugar
8 oz	capers
16 g	oregano *minced*
8 g	thyme *minced*
TT	salt

Place a large rondeau over medium-high heat, add a big squirt of grapeseed oil, and bring to smoking point. Add onions and a couple of pinches of salt. Sauté the onions to get all the water out. Once the steam starts to dissipate, lower the temperature to medium heat. Slowly caramelize the onions but be careful not to burn them. Stir frequently. Once the onions have good color, and fond is starting to form on the bottom of the pan, add in the sugar. It will release a lot of water and help deglaze the onions. Cook down sugar at medium heat for about 10 minutes to cook out some of the moisture from the sugar. Add the rest of the ingredients except for the herbs and cook down for another 10 to 15 minutes. The mixture should look glossy. Pull off the heat and let cool. Once cool, add oregano and thyme, season with salt and more vinegar if needed and cool.

JALAPEÑO CHEVRE

4 lb	chevre, one tub from Pure Luck
9 g	lemon zest
285 g	white distilled vinegar
40 g	pickled jalapeño liquid
140 g	jalapeño ferment
TT	salt and pepper

Place all ingredients in a stand mixer. Whip using white distilled vinegar and olive brine if necessary. If you can't find Pure Luck, add some extra brine. Season with vinegar and if it is too thin use vinegar powder. You can also substitute extra ferment and white distilled vinegar in place of pickled jalapeños. Also keep in mind that some ferments are more spicy than others. Taste first.

PECAN COOKIE

272 g	pecans
132 g	egg whites
284 g	sugar
pinch	sea salt

Place ingredients in a Robot Coupe and incorporate until everything is mixed well and pecans are in small pieces; it should look like lumpy sand. Spread out on a full sheet pan with a Silpat (not parchment), keeping in mind it will only rise a tad. Cook at 350 degrees, low fan for eight minutes. Flip around and cook for another eight minutes. Make sure to spread the mixture on a Silpat evenly and as thin as you can. When mixture is cooked, let cool and put in the dehydrator until it is nice and crispy, which will take a good 30 minutes.

FRIED SHRIMP WITH TASSO-SPICED MAYO & APPLE SLAW

ODD DUCK

We use head-on shrimp for this dish, dredged in a simple mixture of cornmeal and rice flour after soaking the shrimp in buttermilk. Leaving the head on the shrimp really enhances the flavor. Just like a pig head being the most pure pork flavor, the same can be said for the shrimpiest part of the shrimp. Some people can be turned off by the look and aroma of the head, but I always got excited to smell this dish when it came to the pass before heading into the dining room. The mayo is seasoned with a spice mixture that is typically used for spicing pork shoulder before smoking. The apple slaw is a refreshing mix of celery and sesame seeds.

PANTRY STAPLE

TASSO

240 g	black pepper
105 g	white pepper
360 g	sweet paprika
62 g	cayenne
55 g	onion powder
50 g	brown sugar

Toast all the whole spices. Grind until fine in the Vitamix and add in the powdered spices, taste with a little bit of sea salt, package and put away.

GRILLED ZUCCHINI NACHOS

ODD DUCK

I love nachos, but we wanted to make something different than the typical nacho at your favorite Tex-Mex spot. We always try to feature vegetables with our nachos. This version has grilled zucchini with chorizo spices. We use a mix of cheddar and Oaxaca cheese to melt over everything.

At Odd Duck we serve these in a cast iron skillet. The fried tortilla chips are spread out and layered with the veggies and cheese mix over the top before baking in a 400-degree oven. We finish the nachos with fresh herbs, salsa, hot sauce or whatever else works with the seasonal variation.

PANTRY STAPLE

CHORIZO SPICE

13 g	sugar
44 g	paprika
33 g	black pepper
9 g	cinnamon
33 g	coriander
33 g	cumin
3 g	clove
5 g	star anise
9 g	allspice
50 g	New Mexican chile powder

Toast whole spices and then blend and mix with ground spices.

MOTHERS OF INVENTION

Making onion powder at home is oh so easy. Just save your onion peels, dry or dehydrate them, and then pulverize into a powder using a food processor. Jar, label, and store.

PEEL ONION (USE ONION, SAVE SKIN)

DEHYDRATE SKIN

PULVERIZE!!

VEGGIE CHORIZO PRETZEL

ODD DUCK

Adding chorizo spice to veggies fools people into thinking there's real sausage in the mix. This pretzel filling uses zucchini that was still around after Summer, but you could also use other squashes or just the mushrooms.

VEGGIE CHORIZO PRETZEL FILLING

2260 g	button mushroom *grated*
2260 g	zucchini *grated*
165 g	onion
55 g	garlic
232 g	chorizo spice
15 g	oregano *chopped*
65 g	salt
2260 g	cheddar cheese *grated*
250 g	cornstarch

Shred the mushrooms and Oaxaca cheese in a Robot Coupe. Toast the whole spices, then blend and mix charred onion and garlic. Blend and reserve ground spices.

Bake mushrooms and zucchini in oven at 300 degrees until excess moisture is dried out. Remove from oven and mix with cornstarch, salt, and blended onion/garlic. Add chorizo spice and chopped oregano, let cool to room temperature. Mix with shredded Oaxaca cheese. Let cool in fridge.

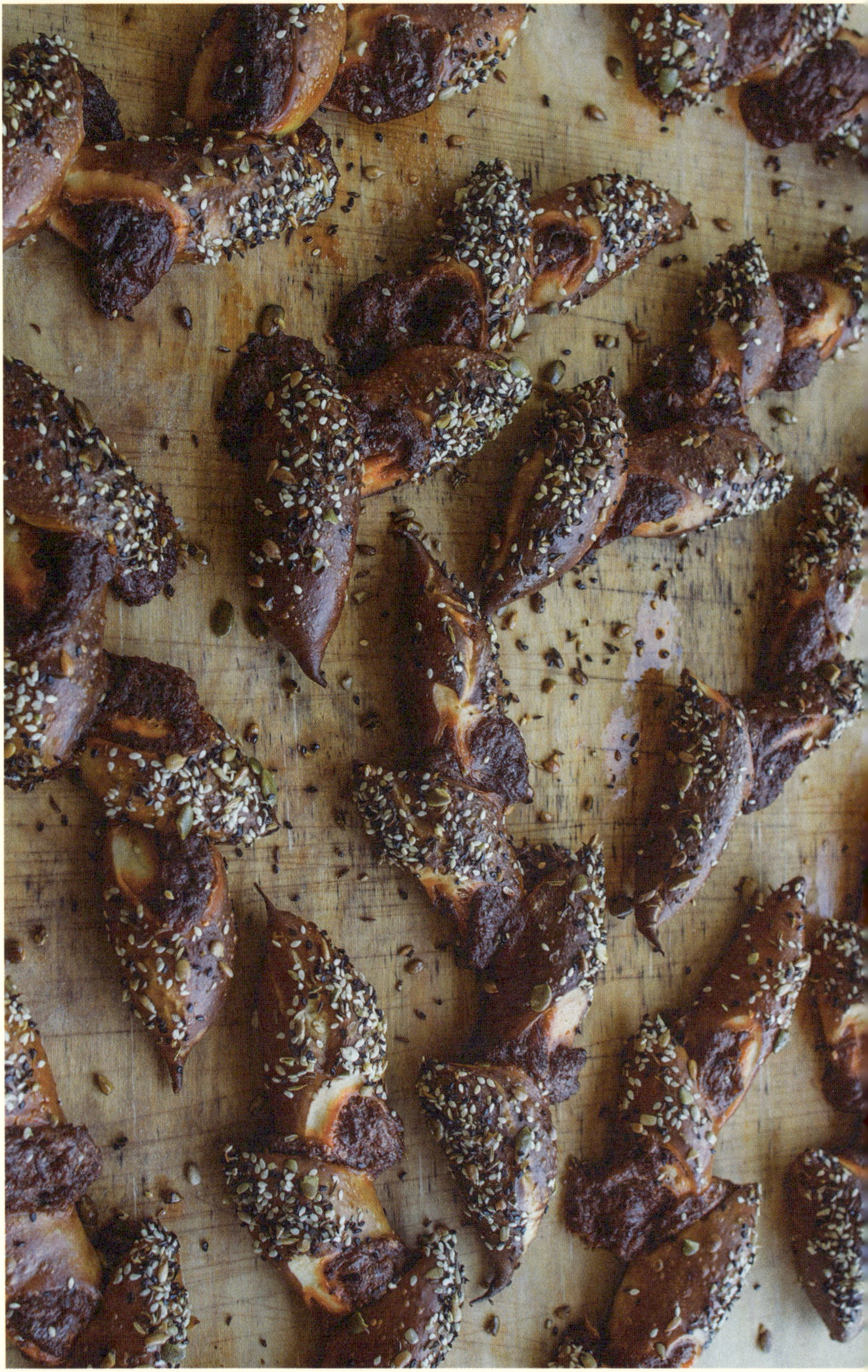

PRETZEL DOUGH

2790 g	milk
2840 g	water
60 g	yeast
9966 g	AP flour
212 g	salt
531 g	butter

STRAIGHT DOUGH METHOD

Mix, rest, shape, retard.

1. Pour the milk and the water into the bowl of a stand mixer. Bloom yeast in milk and water mixture. Sprinkle in flour, salt and softened butter.
2. Mix on speed one for five minutes.
3. Chill dough for shaping the following day.

LYE SOLUTION

26 g	lye
1000 g	water

Dip shaped pretzel 10 seconds each. Lay out the dipped pretzels on a Silpat on a sheet tray. We like to add some kind of seed mix to the top before baking at 450 degrees. Pull from the oven when it's a dark golden-brown and brush it with melted butter. You can reheat and brush with butter again before serving.

HILL COUNTRY SOURDOUGH LOAF

LOAF QTY.	ING.	45	46	47	48	49
%						
80.00	bread flour	17647	18039	18431	18824	19216
20.00	turkey ww	4412	4510	4608	4706	4804
20.00	levain	4412	4510	4608	4706	4804
80.00	water 1	17647	18039	18431	18824	19216
2.00	salt	441	451	461	471	480
2.00	water 2	441	451	461	471	480
204.00		45000	46000	47000	48000	49000

LOAF QTY.	ING.	50	51	52	53	54
%						
80.00	bread flour	19608	20000	20392	20784	21176
20.00	turkey ww	4902	5000	5098	5196	5294
20.00	levain	4902	5000	5098	5196	5294
80.00	water 1	19608	20000	20392	20784	21176
2.00	salt	490	500	510	520	529
2.00	water 2	490	500	510	520	529
204.00		50000	51000	52000	53000	54000

PROCEDURE

Liquids in bottom, dries on top, hold back salt and water 2.

Mix until fully hydrated 4 to 5-min, autolyse 30-min.

After auto, add salt and water 2, adding water gradually.

4 to 5-min. until fully incorporated.

Bulk ferment, fold 3x every 45-min.

Divide 45-min. to 1-hour after last fold, pre-shape round, rest 15 to 30-min.

Final shape, floor proof 30-min. to 1-hour before retarding

COLD TURKEY QUITTER ON SOURDOUGH

SOUR DUCK MARKET

This recipe is a hearty and satisfying sandwich that uses sliced turkey and kale with a cherry bomb dressing on toasted slices of our Hill Country sourdough loaf. Only a few local ranchers raise heritage turkeys in the Fall, and we love to use it exclusively when it's available. At Sour Duck Market, we debone the turkeys but keep the breast meat attached to the leg by the skin. We then roll up each half, so the breast and leg overlap. After smoking, we slice it thin, making sure each slice has a mix of both breast and leg meat.

Kale is another staple of Autumn and can be sourced through most of the Spring. We char the kale quickly before mixing it with the dressing, which pairs well with the chiles and rich egg-y pimento.

CHERRY BOMB DRESSING

500 g	onion *brunoise*
300 g	cherry peppers
8 g	thyme
350 g	Texas olive oil
150 g	apple cider vinegar
275 g	honey
12 g	salt
8 g	black pepper
150 g	Fresno relish
40 g	rice wine vinegar
100 g	pickled mustard seed
8 g	tarragon

Brunoise onion. Heat up onion in 175 grams of the olive oil just until lightly sweaty. Remove from heat and cool in the rest of the olive oil. Blend cherry peppers. Pick and mince tarragon and thyme. Whisk all ingredients together in a mixing bowl.

FRIED EGG PIMENTO CHEESE

60 ea.	soft scrambled eggs
3000 g	shredded cheddar cheese
275 g	minced onion
1300 g	mayo
150 g	Dijon
106 g	capers
20 g	dill
20 g	parsley
20 g	cilantro stem
8 g	black pepper
10 g	paprika
46 g	salt
TT	vinegar

OVEN ROASTED QUAIL WITH OYSTER STUFFING, GRITS, APPLE & MUSTARD GREENS

ODD DUCK

This dish is fitting for the Fall and Thanksgiving time. The apples add a great texture and tartness to cut the richness of the quail and grits. Our favorite apples to use are Honeycrisp. We toss the apples with raw chopped mustard greens and the cider glaze before serving.

Stuff the brined quail as full as possible. Tie the legs together and tuck the wings behind its back. We rub the skin of the quail with butter and spice with tasso. These roast real well in the wood oven. Make sure to rest the bird before cutting in half to show off the stuffing. Finish the whole dish with a drizzle of the glaze.

OYSTER STUFFING

700 g	sourdough *small dice*
400 g	celery *small dice*
400 g	carrots *small dice*
800 g	onions *small dice*
500 g	apples *medium dice*
1 lb	butter
1060 g	raw oysters
900 g	pork belly *medium dice*
32 oz	pork stock
4 oz	white wine
2 oz	Calvados
120 g	parsley stems *small cut*
10 g	tarragon *rough chop*
40 g	chives *small cut*

BREAD. Small dice and bake in the oven at 350 degrees until it is nicely toasted and dried, 10 to 12 minutes.

In a medium-sized pot, melt the butter and sauté the mirepoix with a sachet of thyme and bay leaf. Cook until vegetables are tender. Once vegetables are tender, pour into a mixing bowl and place the pot back on the stove. Place pork belly in the pot and sauté until it gets some color and fond begins to collect at the bottom. Pour the belly pieces into the same mixing bowl as the mirepoix.

Place the pot back on the fire and deglaze with white wine and Calvados. Pour in the pork stock and bring to a boil. Once the stock is to a boil, turn down the heat to medium and pour in the oysters. Slowly poach the oysters and watch for the thinner part of the oyster (the mantle) to begin to curl a little. Pull the oysters out of the stock and allow to cool. Pour the stock mix in with the mirepoix and pork belly one pint at a time until it starts to bind but is not seeping out.

TO FINISH. Add the raw apples, bread, and herbs to the big mixing bowl with the mirepoix. Rough chop the oysters and add them in. Season with salt and cracked black pepper to taste.

GRITS

1500 g	grits	80 g	cream
6 qt	water	1.5 lb	butter *cubed*
.5 gal	milk	150 g	salt
5 gal	buttermilk	TT	pepper

In a large rondeau, bring six quarts of water to a boil. Place grits in a six-quart Cambro or a half hotel pan to rinse. Mix around with water and skim any gritty part of the corn that floats to the top. Repeat until there are no more floaters and strain through a china cap. Slowly add grits to boiling water, whisking pretty hard. Add all other liquid and bring everything back to a boil. A lid will help to speed this up. Return to a simmer and stir every five to 10 minutes for about an hour to an hour and a half. Have a bain marie ready with a spoon to scrape any carpet that wants to form, a spatula to scrape the edge every time, you stir and a whisk. Once cooked about 90%, you can add all of the butter. Whisk until fully incorporated and continue to cook until the grits feel smooth and break down. Season with salt and pepper.

CIDER GLAZE FOR QUAIL

1000 g	apple jus
1000 g	apple cider vinegar
600 g	raw sugar
230 g	water
300 g	coffee *brewed*
2 g	cloves
2 g	anise
2 ea.	Vietnamese cinnamon
4 g	black cardamom
20 g	Urfa biber
TT	salt

Make a caramel with the sugar and the water. Wait until the caramel turns amber and add the vinegar. Use the vinegar to stop the caramel. Don't use anything else or you will burn it. Add the rest of the ingredients and reduce by half. Season with salt, pass through a wooden handle strainer and cool.

GOAT STROGANOFF, BOILED PEANUT, SWEET POTATO & LEMON KALE

BARLEY SWINE

This is a satisfying, hearty dish that combines goat and sweet potatoes. The fried potato skins add great texture and the boiled peanut broth ties everything together. Most of our peanuts come from Texas farms that grow a Spanish variety. We buy them in the shell and peel them ourselves, but this broth takes on flavor from boiling the peanuts in their shell.

ROSEMARY OIL
100 g	kale *blanched (weigh before blanching)*
40 g	picked rosemary
2 g	thyme
300 g	grapeseed oil

Blend and filter strain.

> **MAMA SAID**
> Use the **BOIL SPICE** pantry staple from page 68 to boil your peanuts, or any other thing you're boiling, for that matter.

BOILED PEANUTS. Take 150 grams of **BOIL SPICE** and add it to eight quarts of water. Bring to a boil and boil spice. Then add local peanuts and cook for two to four hours.

GOAT BRAISING. Debone goat shoulders. Season with 1% salt. Roll and tie shoulders. Rub the outside with boil spice. Slowly grill goat over low flames or coal until golden-brown and delicious, not too charred. Place in a hotel pan with hot goat stock to cover half to two thirds of the goat. Cover with lid. Braise for four to six hours until a cake tester easily slides in and out.

LEMON KALE. Tear kale into bite size pieces. Toss the kale in a lemon oil and salt to taste. Then Cryovac for at least 30 minutes.

PICKLE RELISH
    2 parts boiled peanuts
    1 part okra
    1 part pickled kale stem
    3 parts apple vinegar
    2 parts water
    1 part sugar

Cut to like-sized pieces. Mix and season with lemon juice, lemon oil, and Microplaned ginger.

GOAT JUS. Reduce braise liquid until seasoned, not salty. If it is not glazed enough, thicken with some xanthan gum.

SWEET POTATOES. Pan-fry split sweet potatoes skin-on in goat fat until al dente. Cool to room temperature. Peel skins and reserve for garnish crispies. Oblique cut potatoes into 1 in. × 1 in. cubes. Fry skins at 300 degrees and season with sea salt.

RECIPES FOR AUTUMN

GOAT STROGANOFF GLAZE

400 g	goat jus
400 g	yogurt
1 g	picked thyme
5 g	picked rosemary
40 g	chile brine
±5 g	xanthan gum

Blend yogurt, thyme, rosemary, and brine first. Then stream in the melted jus and the xanthan gum to your desired texture. Be aware that xanthan changes thickness with room temp. Strain through a chinois and season.

PEANUT BROTH

316 g	lightly toasted peanuts
1,120 g	boil liquid
912 g	bok choy ferment
1,700 g	goat stock or water
20 g	juniper
20 g	rosemary
20 g	thyme
5 ea.	garlic cloves smashed
10 g	MSG
TT	boil powder

Combine peanuts, boil liquid, ferment, and stock in pot and bring to boil. Add aromatics and steep for 45 minutes. Pull out aromatics and blend the liquid for a long lime to incorporate the nuts. Strain through a chinois and season to taste.

RYE PECAN CAKE

SOUR DUCK MARKET

1609 g	sugar
585 g	rye flour
47 g	baking powder
702 g	pecan meal
24 g	salt
732 g	butter
732 g	brown butter
1463 g	egg whites

Sift sugar, rye, and baking powder together. Combine sifted dries with pecan meal and salt using the paddle attachment and stand mixer. Melt butters together to 149 degrees. Bring whites up to 90 degrees. Add half of the whites to dries. Stream in the remaining whites in six installments. Once incorporated and shininess has dulled, stream in butters. Wait until incorporated before adding more. Scoop into buttered muffin pans and top with pecans before baking at 350 degrees in a convection oven.

The ORIGIN Story

OR HOW IT ALL BEGAN...

BY BRYCE GILMORE

THIS WHOLE THING started in 2009, around Springtime. I was working in Aspen at The Little Nell with Mark David Buley and Sam Hellman-Mass, and I was feeling an itch to move back to my hometown of Austin, Texas. I had reached a point of not wanting to work for another chef, but also wasn't in a position to buy a restaurant. I've always had an entrepreneurial spirit, and I really like being in charge so naturally, I wanted to own a business someday.

Then the thought occurred to me, what about a food truck? They were super popular in Austin at the time and the investment and risk were minimal. I also noticed more and more people were going to farmer's markets and in general, being more mindful about where their food was coming from. I thought these two ideas paired well and so the idea for a farm-to-truck concept was born. I told Mark, Sam, and the chef at The Little Nell I was going to move to Austin and open a food trailer. Of course, they all thought I was crazy, but I didn't care because it felt right. At the time, the rest of the country hadn't entirely caught onto food trailers yet and Austin was at the forefront of the craze.

"IT WAS A 1980'S FLEETWOOD MALLARD COVERED IN DUCKS AND NAMED LAURA'S WEINER WAGON."

I left Colorado that July and by September had found an old, used trailer on eBay. It was a 1980's Fleetwood Mallard covered in painted ducks and named Laura's Weiner Wagon. I thought about having a trailer custom made, but it would have been a big white box on wheels. A lot of people were fixing up Airstreams at the time, and I looked into that too, but I wanted something with even more character and the Mallard trailer was precisely that. It had already lived a life or two by the time I found it, one of which inspired my wife to dub our venture Odd Duck.

I had quite the time picking up the trailer from Wisconsin, and even got pulled over and searched by the police in Missouri on a highway known for drug trafficking. When I finally made it back to Austin, my brother Dylan and I gutted the trailer and spent three-months renovating while we also scoped out choice spots to park. At the time, Gourdough's was in the space right next to where Odd Duck now lives. There seemed to be plenty of room for more, so I tracked down the owner and convinced him to let us put the trailer there, and it ended up staying there for two years.

Early Odd Duck Farm to Trailer crew, (L-R) Jon, Hilary, Dylan and Bryce.

Laura's Weiner Wagon made over into Odd Duck Farm to Trailer and a detail of its daily menu board.

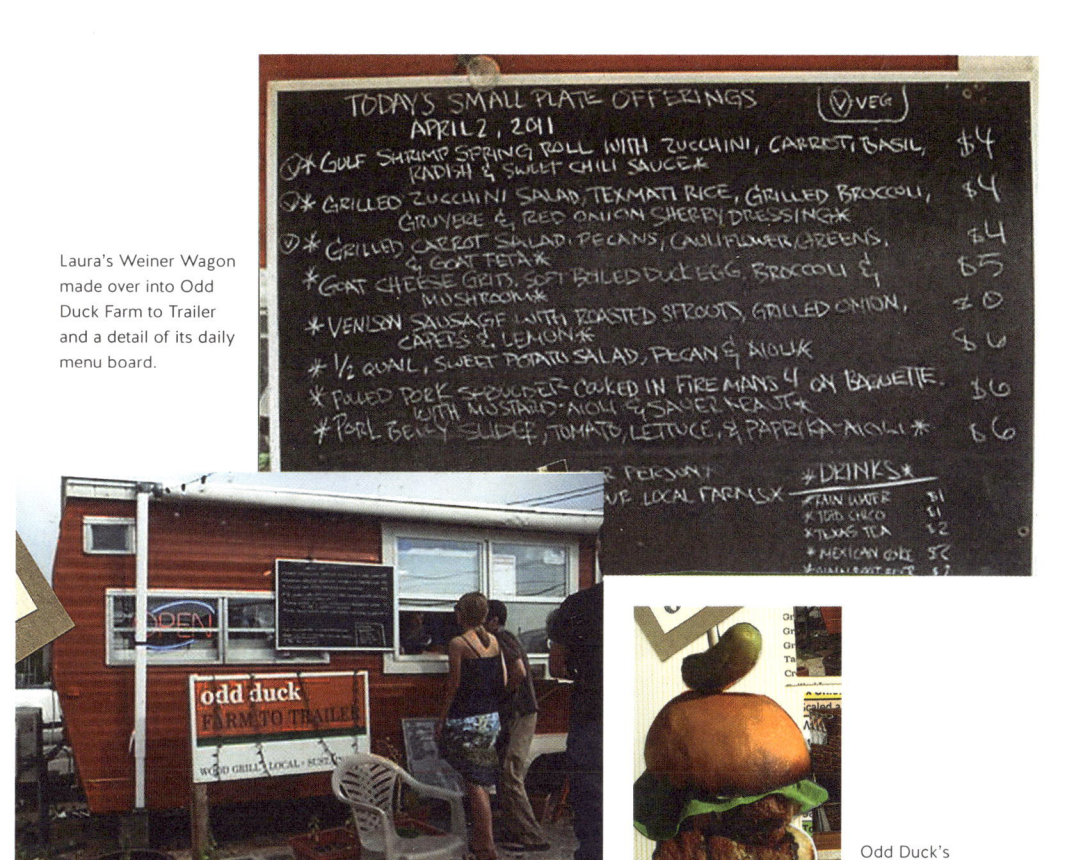

Odd Duck's famous pork belly slider.

Initially, I wanted to do a small plate concept because I liked the idea of being able to try everything—even ordering the whole menu if you wanted. All the ingredients were sourced from local farms and cooked on a four foot long wood-burning grill that I found on Craigslist for a steal. That same grill is still powering the Odd Duck brick and mortar restaurant to this day.

We opened the trailer that December when it was freezing outside, and weren't getting a ton of business at first. There was no real social media presence, it was all word of mouth, and we slowly started to gain traction with positive local write-ups. Then all of a sudden, the producers for *No Reservations* called us and wanted to feature Odd Duck on an episode with Anthony Bourdain. Obviously, after that, things took off quickly. We did a couple of other Food Network shows, like *The Best Thing You Ever Ate*, which featured our pork belly slider.

THE ORIGIN STORY

Bryce, Marsh, and Gabe in the Odd Duck kitchen.

Two early dishes from Odd Duck.

> "IT WAS A LOT OF LONG DAYS, BUT IT WAS FUN BECAUSE WE WERE DOING WHAT WE WANTED."

Later that first year, I noticed an old pie shop was for lease down the street. When I saw the space, I immediately thought gastropub because it was such a popular concept at the time, and I liked the idea of a bar with a full menu. So, in August of 2010, I signed a lease and started shifting my focus from the trailer to opening my first brick and mortar restaurant.

We opened Barley Swine that December, just a year after the trailer had opened and we were faced with the decision of whether to close the trailer or try to run both at the same time. Dylan decided he would keep the trailer going with the staff we already had so I could focus one hundred percent on opening Barley Swine. Sam Hellman-Mass came down to visit from Chicago, where he had moved after leaving Aspen and I asked him to be a part of the restaurant. One of the guys from the trailer, Jon, was my other sous chef. It was just the three of us at first, but we slowly started adding other cooks. It was a lot of long days, but it was fun because we were doing what we wanted.

Barley Swine started to evolve into this higher-end concept around the same time we had to close the Odd Duck trailer because our lot had been purchased by developers for the construction of a new apartment building. Also, our team had developed to where I thought it would be a good idea to open Odd Duck in a larger space with a lower price point. It's at this time that Mark David Buley came down and joined us in anticipation of the opening.

We opened the restaurant version of Odd Duck in December of 2013. It's easy to remember because we somehow always open our new concepts in December. The entire opening menu featured our favorite dishes from over the years. I remember people commenting on that, and I said, "No shit, it's our first menu, we want to do food we know works!"

As our three-year mark approached at Barley Swine, we got into some lease drama with our landlord and started looking for other spaces. At the time it made sense to go bigger and open in a different part of town. In 2016, we opened Barley Swine 2.0 on Burnet Road. At first, Barley Swine had an a la carte menu only. The concept was to order two to three dishes per person, but then we switched to a full-on tasting menu and were actually one of the first places in Austin to offer a tasting menu only. We ran service like that for about two years. I built the new kitchen to execute both a tasting menu and an a la carte menu because I thought it would be

Barley Swine 2.0 on Burnet Road.

> **"IT'S HARD TO BELIEVE WE STARTED AS A FOOD TRUCK TEN YEARS AGO AND NOW WE HAVE THREE STOREFRONTS."**

cool for people to have a choice. We have two totally separate menus, which can be challenging to execute, but I think it works out for everyone.

I'm the only operating partner at Barley Swine, and I was satisfied between that and Odd Duck. However, the other partners (Dylan, Mark, and Jason James) wanted to do something else and honestly, it just made sense because Odd Duck was crazy busy at the time. We decided to open an off-site bakery where we could bake our bread and also an extra kitchen for butchering. We found an existing catering kitchen, on the Eastside with a little café and a big backyard with overgrown citrus trees and a couple of old structures attached to it.

Some things you plan, and some things just naturally evolve. Sour Duck Market happened because of timing. The availability of that particular place and the team we had at the time made it all happen. It made sense for Mark to take over the Sour Duck Market project because of his background, but we also wanted managers to

Cody, Parker, and Mark in the Sour Duck Market bakery.

An Odd Duck workday at Phoenix Farms in Bastrop. (L-R) Casey, Nate (farm-owner), Stefan, Richard, Katon, Christy, and Rebecca.

be able to move around—to keep learning and growing. We've only hired one sous chef from outside the company, but other than that, they've all been employees we've trained and promoted in-house.

This takes us to right now. This is who we are, and these are the people who are creating delicious food, drink, and hospitality for you. We've got the best people, and that's what keeps the place running. It's hard to believe we started as a food truck ten years ago and now we have three storefronts. This restaurant group has seen a lot of great people come and go, both staff and guests.

People often ask what we're all about, what's our story? I sum it up like this; we have a straightforward concept and philosophy focused on creating menus with what we can find in and around Austin and Texas. We're also transparent about our ingredients' origins and like to celebrate the farmers and fine folks behind them. But the bigger picture's not about Mark or me or Dylan or Jason; it's about the representation of a particular place at a specific time and the talented people making it happen.

THE ORIGIN STORY

FROM THE BREWERY

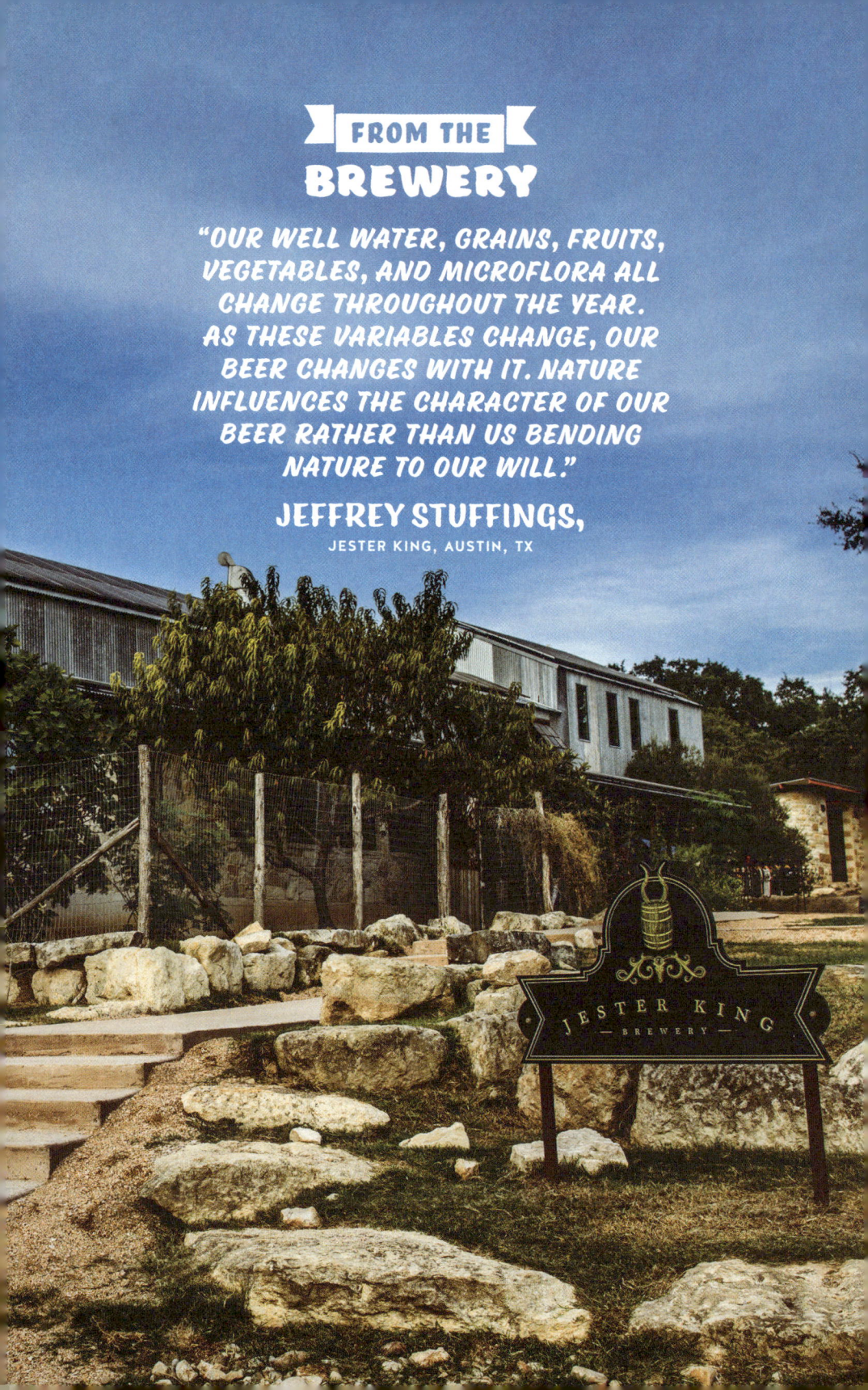

"OUR WELL WATER, GRAINS, FRUITS, VEGETABLES, AND MICROFLORA ALL CHANGE THROUGHOUT THE YEAR. AS THESE VARIABLES CHANGE, OUR BEER CHANGES WITH IT. NATURE INFLUENCES THE CHARACTER OF OUR BEER RATHER THAN US BENDING NATURE TO OUR WILL."

JEFFREY STUFFINGS,
JESTER KING, AUSTIN, TX

RECIPES FROM THE BAR

DRINKS

YEAR ROUND

THAT OLD LIQUID SUNSHINE

PERENNIAL SAUCE!
THIS MUST BE WHAT THEY MEANT BY
AMBER WAVES OF GRAIN.

OUR CELEBRATION of the Texas bounty extends beyond the kitchens and into the bar programs. We put the same ingredients that are in season into liquid form, resulting in drinks like carrot mules, beet Bloody Marys and cognac cocktails sweetened with sunchoke simple syrup. Part of the reason our restaurants remain as close to zero-waste as possible is because our bar chefs find ways to creatively turn scraps and byproducts into syrups, bitters and infused spirits (case in point: fried chicken tequila). They'll bounce ideas off the kitchen staff, team up with the restaurants' pastry chefs to craft garnishes, and they're even handy with a dang Cryovac. We also love to support area distillers who work in small batches and produce their spirits using sustainable and local ingredients like non-GMO corn (Still Austin whiskey) and West Texas desert spoon plant (Desert Door sotol). Because you should always be thinking about what you're drinking too.

NO BRAINER

ODD DUCK

1.5 oz	Vida Mezcal
.5 oz	Velvet Falernum
.75 oz	lime juice
.75 oz	spicy agave simple syrup
1 oz	watermelon
1 oz	Brut Rosé

Pour one ounce of Brut Rosé into a large coupe. In shaker tin, combine the rest of the ingredients. Shake and strain into the coupe. Garnish with water-melon wedge.

BAR STAPLE

SPICY AGAVE SIMPLE SYRUP

Combine two quarts agave and two quarts water into a pan. As it's warming, add eight sliced Thai chiles (test how spicy the chile is before adding). Bring this all to a boil and immediately remove from heat. Allow to steep as it returns to room temperature. Strain and refrigerate.

TRINIDAD JOKES

ODD DUCK

1.5 oz.	Dripping Springs vodka
1.5 oz.	cantaloupe juice
.75 oz.	lemon
.5 oz.	Damiana
.5 oz.	Trinidad honey

Add all ingredients into a shaker tin with ice. Shake and double strain over small cubes in a Collins glass. Slapped tarragon to garnish.

BAR STAPLE

TRINIDAD HONEY

500 g	honey
500 g	water
70 g	Trinidad peppers *chopped & destemmed*

Bring ingredients to a boil and let sit at room temp until cool. Strain and reserve Trinidad pieces to put on your pizza when you get home.

PALOMA

ODD DUCK

A staple on draft whenever we can get local Texas grapefruits. People get angry when we take it off the menu during the Summer months when grapefruits aren't available.

1.75 oz.	silver tequila
.25 oz.	aperol
1 oz.	grapefruit juice
.5 oz.	lime
.1 oz	ginger
.75 oz.	tarragon simple syrup
.5 oz.	soda water

BAR STAPLE

TARRAGON SIMPLE SYRUP

Combine four quarts organic sugar, 4-quarts of water and 75 grams of chopped tarragon into a pan. Bring to a boil and immediately remove from heat. Allow to steep as it returns to room temperature. Strain and refrigerate.

RECIPES FROM THE BAR

SALT OF THE EARTH COCKTAIL

ODD DUCK

We like to incorporate seasonal produce into the cocktails at Odd Duck. Fruit seems like a logical pairing but sometimes the veggies need their chance to shine. I'm a big fan of gin to begin with, and I will always love it with beets after trying this drink.

BEET SHRUB. Take 10 whole beets and toss them in grapeseed oil, wrap them in foil and roast at 350 degrees for one hour (or until soft).

Allow to cool enough to handle and peel by rubbing the beets with a towel. Cut into eighths and coat in equal parts by weight with sugar. Macerate at room temp with cheesecloth cover overnight. The next day add equal parts white balsamic. Cover and refrigerate. Strain for use.

BAR STAPLE

TARRAGON & BLACK PEPPER OIL

Heat three ounces of black pepper kernels in a saucepan. Add one bunch of chopped tarragon and toasted peppercorns. Cool and transfer to one cup of olive oil in a container. Let sit for at least three days and strain.

COCKTAIL

1.25 oz	Ransom gin
.25 oz	Lustau sherry
.5 oz	green chartreuse
.75 oz	beet shrub
5 drops	tarragon & black pepper oil

Stir in tin until well-chilled. Strain into coupe. Add five drops of tarragon & black pepper oil.

CORY'S COFFEE

ODD DUCK

1.5 oz	Clyde Mays bourbon
.25 oz	Dolin dry vermouth
.5 oz	cinnamon & vanilla simple syrup (pg. 150)
1 oz	cold brew coffee

Combine all ingredients in a pint glass with ice, stir, and strain over a large rock. Garnish with orange peel.

RECIPES FROM THE BAR

WHISKEY 'N CIDER

ODD DUCK

1.25 oz	Clyde Mays
.5 oz	Calvados
.25 oz	Benedictine
.25 oz	lemon juice
.25 oz	cinnamon & vanilla simple syrup
1.5 oz	apple cider
3 drops	salt brine
garnish	apple wedge

APPLE CIDER. Wash and core apples (use a blend of apples if available). Juice, strain, and cover with cheese cloth secured with a rubber band. Let sit for 24 hours and strain again. Good for four to five days in the fridge.

BAR STAPLE

CINNAMON & VANILLA SIMPLE SYRUP

6 c	water
8 c	organic sugar
2 c	Vietnamese cinnamon chips
2 ea.	vanilla beans (scrape out most of the middle of the bean)

Bring to a boil slowly. When it starts to boil, turn off the heat and let it cool in the pan slowly.

barley SWINE
odd duck
sour duck

DIRECT FROM THE MOTHER SHIP

THE FOLKS who work at Odd Duck, Barley Swine, and Sour Duck Market are a family. With that comes love, respect, and camaraderie, but also conflicts, failures, and gossip. Here are some notable quotes heard around the kitchen that give insight into the culture and relationships that drive these ever-inventive culinary establishments.

> I THINK IT'S CUTE THOSE OF US IN SALARIED MANAGERIAL ROLES HAVE PARENTAL NICKNAMES. THE OTHER PARTNERS AND I ARE PAPAS, THE MANAGERS ARE MOMS AND DADS, AND THE STAFF MEMBERS ARE LOVINGLY REFERRED TO AS SQUIRRELS.
>
> **JASON JAMES,**
> PARTNER & GENERAL MANAGER

"SQUIRREL," COMES

from when I worked at Perry's Steak House about eight years ago. One of the head servers always hid random things in different areas of the restaurant and moved super fast and abruptly ALL the time. I adopted it as a term of endearment for him, and it has been with me ever since—and now it has become a part of the Odd Duck vernacular!

CHRISTINE REGAN,
ASSISTANT GENERAL MANAGER, ODD DUCK

WE HAVE AN EMPLOYEE

who has been with us for nearly six years named Jennifer. She is famous for saying she, "wants guests to taste a dish before they taste it." She works for me as a server at Barley Swine now, where her name is programmed in our computer system as "Taste It."

STEFAN DAVIS,

GENERAL MANAGER,
BARLEY SWINE

I LOVE THAT OUR CHEFS can take a feeling, a moment, a speck of time from their lives, and turn it into an elevated dish that invokes a similar nostalgia in everyone who eats that dish. When I first started, Mark Buley made a version of what his brother used to cook him as a kid: macaroni with sliced hot dogs. But Mark's version was a "tootsie roll" pasta stuffed with pork and quail sausage. It was amazing. I've been hooked on Odd Duck ever since.

JUSTIN BURTON,
MANAGER AND BEER DUDE,
ODD DUCK

ONE OF MY FAVORITE MOMENTS FROM WORKING AT ODD DUCK, HAS TO BE MARK DAVID BULEY WRESTLING ANYONE TO GET HIS WAY.

CHRISTIAN GARCIA,
CHEF DE CUISINE, ODD DUCK

DIRECT FROM THE MOTHER SHIP

WHENEVER SOMEONE was looking for something in the restaurant and they would ask around, one of our best line cooks (Nick Leyva) would always reply with the question: "Did you check up your butt?" Nick moved on to another city a year ago. But to this day, we often use "Did you check up your butt?" in the same context. It's like Michael Scott and "that's what she said."

ZECH PEREZ,
CHEF DE CUISINE, SOUR DUCK

I USED TO BE A PICKY eater, but have grown less so the longer I work here. Bryce has a way of changing my mind about ingredients I would otherwise avoid. I hate mayo, but he once had a dish on the menu with sausage and pancakes and coffee mayo that was a game-changer!

LINDSAY SATTLER,
ASSISTANT GENERAL MANAGER, BARLEY SWINE

156

THE ODD DUCK ALMANAC

MY FAVORITE MEMORY IS FROM WHEN I FIRST STARTED HERE AND WE WERE PREPPING OUR STATIONS ON THE DINING ROOM TABLES BECAUSE THE KITCHEN WAS SO SMALL.

KEVIN CANNON,
CHEF DE CUISINE, BARLEY SWINE

SOMEONE CAME IN for dinner in their Ferrari and left the vehicle (and the key) with the valet overnight. The next day, they picked up their car with another key and so we had a random Ferrari key laying around. Mark Buley attached the key to some butcher twine and every night a bad-ass back of house employee is awarded the Ferrari key necklace for wearing during the remainder of the evening.

NICK BLOOMINGDALE,
MANAGER AND BEER BUYER, SOUR DUCK MARKET

B5
Estiva
Beorange
Cherokee Purple
Amazing heirloom tomato that tops most
lists for true tomato flavor and color

Sour Duck
FARMER'S MARKET

"YOUNG PEOPLE AND ANYONE INTERESTED IN FARMING SHOULD BE ABLE TO CONSIDER IT A VIABLE CAREER OPTION."

ONE OF MY GOALS is to help small-scale farmers thrive. We started a Wednesday evening farmer's market at Sour Duck because we wanted to provide a place for farmers to sell their products with minimal risk during the week. All the other farmer's markets in town have a booth fee, so if there's bad weather or a poor turnout, they might not make a lot of money. We invite local farmers to sell their produce with no fees, and we also buy their perishables that won't make it to the next market for use in our kitchens.

LEFT
Jamey of B5 Farms in Lockhart, Texas.

ABOVE
Sam and Marisa selling pickles and kimchi.

EVERY WEDNESDAY 4PM-7PM (OR 'TIL SOLD OUT!)
SOUR DUCK Farmers Market
Farm Fresh
LOCAL FARMERS BRINGING THEIR GOODS TO YOUR 'HOOD!
Come support your local market
LIVE MUSIC STARTS AT 5PM
SOUR DUCK MARKET
1814 EAST MLK JR BLVD
AUSTIN, TX 78702

Young people and anyone interested in farming should be able to consider it a viable career option. For that to happen, more venues are needed for them to sell their products. Right now, there's too much risk involved. The work can be grueling, and most farmers don't even have health insurance. If there's a bad storm and it knocks down your barn or your coop flies away, there needs to be some fund to recover.

Texas Farmers Market has an agricultural support program in place for the farmers who sell at their market, which is cool, and Slow Food Austin raises money to assist farmers in recovering from loss and damage too. There are so many great food organizations doing great things in Austin, but somebody needs to bring it all together. There's a lot of room for improvement in helping out small farmers.

TOP The backyard of Sour Duck during a farmer's market. String Theory, plays a set in the old Odd Duck Farm to Trailer made over into a stage.

BOTTOM Katon, a manager at Sour Duck bagging some produce.

FACING Promotional poster by Brock Caron.

DIRECT FROM THE MOTHER SHIP

ODD DUCK

1201 S Lamar Blvd
Austin, TX 78704
foh@oddduckaustin.com
512-433-6521
oddduckaustin.com

BARLEY SWINE

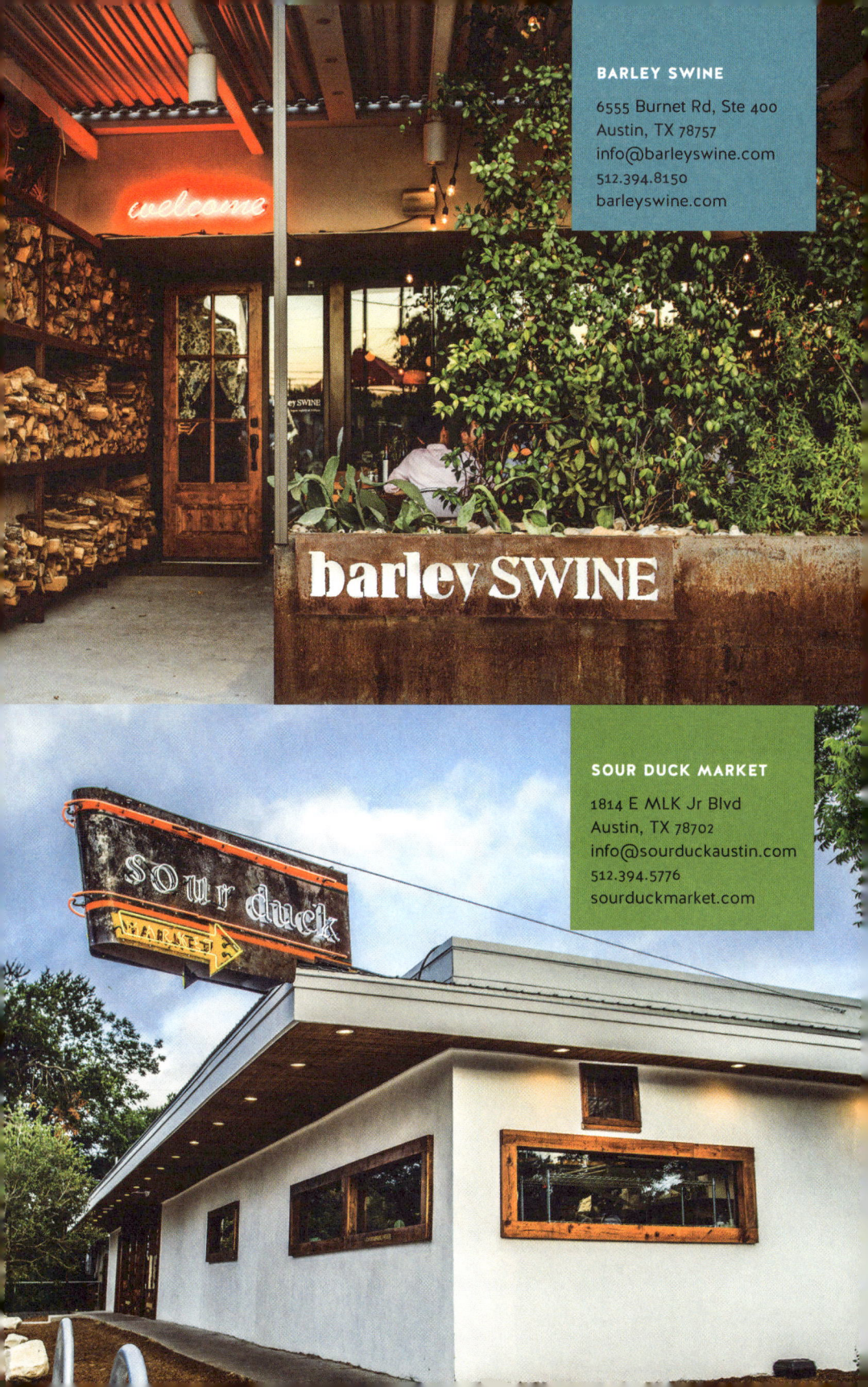

6555 Burnet Rd, Ste 400
Austin, TX 78757
info@barleyswine.com
512.394.8150
barleyswine.com

SOUR DUCK MARKET

1814 E MLK Jr Blvd
Austin, TX 78702
info@sourduckaustin.com
512.394.5776
sourduckmarket.com

The Odd Duck Almanac
Copyright © 2020 by Cattywampus Press

All rights reserved
Printed in USA
First edition

No part of this book may be reproduced or utilized in any form or by any means, electronic or mechanical, including photocopying, recordings or by any information storage and retrieval system without permission in writing from the publisher:
    Cattywampus Press
    7421 Burnet Road, #164
    Austin, TX 78210
    contact@cattywampuspress.com

Quote from Cas Van Woerden (pg. 30) courtesy of animalfarmcenter.com

ISBN 978-1-7340625-1-9

Design and typesetting by Lindsay Starr.
Printed, bound, and distributed by OneTouchPoint, Austin.

Publicity by Resplendent Hospitality, Austin.